MEL BAY'S COMPLETE JAZZ GUITARIST

By Jimmy Stewart

A cassette tape of the music in this book is now available. The publisher strongly recommends the use of this cassette tape along with the text to insure accuracy of interpretation and ease in learning.

Music In The Style Of

Django Reinhardt

Wes Montgomery

T-Bone Walker

Larry Carlton

Pat Metheny

Stanley Jordan

And Many More....

Special Thanks

Apophis Music Production

Bill Bay

Scott Yanow

Gretchen Horton Hopper

George Adjieff

GHS Strings

Coda Music Software

TABLE OF CONTENTS

ABOUT THE BOOK

In this book you will learn the influential styles that have revolutionized jazz guitar playing. Each style of composition portrays that unique musical signature created by the guitar personality featured.

Designed for the guitarist at any level, each song shows string indications, music and fingering notation. A special chapter, *The History of Jazz Guitar*, by jazz columnist/historian Scott Yanow, explains the influential and important musical styles of many jazz guitarists.

The chapter tips and ideas present a series of principles to reinforce a basic understanding of jazz guitar techniques.

The recording accompanying this book will act as an interface between the printed music and the guitarist.

Finally, an appendix explains musicians' symbols, the mechanics of guitar playing and guidelines for listening. The comprehensive *Evolution of Jazz Guitar chart* can be used as a quick guide for locating time frames and styles.

With applied study of this book and recording both the beginner and experienced player will have developed a better understanding of the wide range of jazz guitar.

Jimmy Stewart

ABOUT THE AUTHOR

Jimmy Stewart is a master of the guitar with over 1,200 recordings to his credit; besides recording, his impressive accomplishments include writing, teaching, composing, and, of course, working full time in a band on the road. As a prolific writer of books and magazine articles and through his decade-long, popular columns in *Guitar Player Magazine*, he has taught and influenced millions of musicians around the world. In 1991 Jimmy was inducted into the *Jazz Hall of Fame*.

Stewart plays virtuously all styles of guitar—from classical to hard rock. However, like many musicians, his first instinctive love is jazz.

This book reveals how this fine guitarist plays and thinks about jazz guitar.

William Bay

THE HISTORY OF JAZZ GUITAR

The guitar, today the dominant instrument in pop and rock music, was actually a minor force in jazz until the late 1920s. Because of its mobility, the guitar was most often used in the early days by country blues singers and itinerant folk minstrels to accompany their vocals as they roamed the South in search of work. In the New Orleans jazz bands of the pre-1930 era, the banjo was actually preferred over the guitar due to its louder volume.

While the guitar became such a prominent part of the blues world that one cannot imagine such singers/ musicians as Leadbelly, Blind Blake and Lonnie Johnson performing in the early days without their instruments, it was not until the rise of Eddie Lang that jazz had its first jazz guitarist of real prominence. Known for his purity of tone, his graceful swinging phrases and his sophisticated chord voicing, Lang often teamed up with violinist Joe Venuti and was a part of a countless number of recordings up until his premature death in 1933. Lang's work included duets with fellow guitarists Lonnie Johnson and Carl Kress, accompaniments to blues singers such as Bessie Smith and many commercial dates.

With the development of the electric microphone and the subsequent vast improvement in recording techniques, the acoustic guitar completely replaced the banjo by the early 1930s. But the guitar, which became a part of nearly every swing band of the decade, was still primarily used as a rhythmic background instrument. Carl Kress, Dick McDonough and the still active George Van Eps extended the legacy of Eddie Lang, developing their own chordal approaches, but solo opportunities were rare. More typical were the roles of Allan Reuss with Benny Goodman's Big Band and Freddie Green with Count Basie Orchestra as important but barely audible members of the rhythm section who provided an airy, elastic foundation for the driving 4/4 beat of these influential bands of the swing era.

While Big Bill Broonzy and Blind Willie McTell were major soloists in the blues world, the Belgian gypsy Django Reinhardt, playing with the Quintet of the Hot Club of France, was among the very first in jazz to play the guitar primarily as a solo instrument, a role formerly reserved for horn players and pianists. It greatly helped that Django performed not with a big band but with violinist Stephane Grappelli, two rhythm guitars and a bass; there was never any problem hearing him in that setting. Django's solos were brilliantly constructed and synthesized the two elements of single-string leads and chord solos.

George M. Smith brought the guitar to prominence in motion picture scores (such as *The Grapes Of Wrath, Young Mr. Lincoln* and *Tobacco Road*), showing many European composers the great range of colors, styles and moods of which the guitar was capable, but it took the advent of the electrically amplified guitar to lift the instrument out of the rhythm section and into the solo spotlight. While the genius Les Paul had experimented with building an electric guitar almost a decade earlier, Eddie Durham (with a small group of Count Basie sidemen) took a few early electric guitar solos in 1938 and Floyd Smith (with Andy Kirk's Orchestra) had been showcased on *"Floyd's Guitar Blues"* (although his Hawaiian effects make this more of a novelty than an innovation), it would be up to Charlie Christian to upgrade the guitar to the level of a horn.

Featured throughout his all-too-brief career mostly with the Benny Goodman Sextet, Christian's clean lines, natural swing and logical ideas allowed him to hold his own with the likes of Benny Goodman, Lionel Hampton and trumpeter Cootie Williams; he even jammed at after-hours nightclubs with the young Dizzy Gillespie and Thelonious Monk. Charlie Christian's solos, which bridged the gap between swing and bop, became so influential that it would be 20 years before jazz guitar advanced much beyond his style of phrasing.

Even with Christian being the main influence on guitarists during the 1940s, '50s and into the '60s, other musicians with individual conceptions of their own emerged. T-Bone Walker was the Charlie Christian of the blues world, George Barnes played both jazz and blues on electric guitar in what would formerly have been acoustic settings, and Barney Kessel in the mid-'40s, performing with both swing big bands and bop combos, was sometimes thought of as the "new Charlie Christian." Kessel, Jimmy Raney, Tal Farlow, Herb

Ellis and Kenny Burrell all led many small group recording sessions from the 1950s on, an unheard-of situation prior to Christian; each guitarist eventually developed his own distinctive voice within the Charlie Christian tradition. In addition, Les Paul's popular recordings, both with and without Mary Ford, showed the enormous potential of the electric guitar sound.

And yet, the acoustic guitar did not completely disappear. By the 1950s the guitar (both electric and acoustic) had become widely accepted in the studio, where men such as the chordal-based Johnny Smith lent their sounds anonymously to commercial backgrounds, and with individuality on their own recordings; his *"Moonlight In Vermont"* became a major hit of the era. Laurindo Almeida with Stan Kenton's Orchestra showed how an acoustic classical guitar could fit into a jazz setting and, as the 1960s began, Charlie Byrd, along with tenor-saxophonist Stan Getz fused together Brazilian rhythms with a classical sound and jazz improvisation to form bossa nova.

In the first half of the 1960s, the Charlie Christian style remained dominant. Wes Montgomery amazed listeners with his fast octaves, Grant Green excelled in both straight ahead bop and some funkier jazz. By the end of the decade, George Benson became the last major new exponent of the Christian sound, adding his own personality to the style of nearly 30 years before.

The advent of rock in the late 1960s made it clear that it was only a matter of time before the jazz guitar would be affected. While B.B. King was now the dominant guitarist in blues, Mike Bloomfield brought the electric guitar sound to rock; eventually the major rock guitarist Jimi Hendrix would give both blues and jazz guitarists a new option, using distortion along with advanced improvising skills to create individual sounds that owed little to Charlie Christian.

In jazz Larry Coryell, at first playing with vibraphonist Gary Burton's group, brought the sound of electric blues rock into jazz. Gabor Szabo (whose music reflected his Hungarian legacy), Sonny Sharrock (who played rockish guitar in an avant-garde setting) and Pat Martino (coming from the bop tradition) were open to the influence of rock, but it was John McLaughlin, at first with Miles Davis and Tony Williams Lifetime, and particularly with his own Mahavishnu Orchestra, who brought the guitar into fusion, combining the sound and power of rock with the sophisticated improvisations of jazz. Following in his wake was the virtuosic speed demon Al DiMeola with *Return to Forever*; both McLaughlin and DiMeola have remained major influences on rock guitarists interested in jazz up to the present time. Most consider Stevie Ray Vaughan, a blues man who really developed the Jimi Hendrix sound, as their equivalent in blues.

But even with the dominance of the many fusion guitarists, the acoustic and bop styles have not disappeared. In fact the 1980s were most notable for the many different approaches that could be taken in playing jazz guitar. Both McLaughlin and DiMeola spent much of their time playing acoustically, Ralph Towner (often with Oregon) displayed the influence of folk music, and Earl Klugh brought an easy-listening sound to the jazz world. Larry Carlton and Lee Ritenour on electric guitar displayed both pop music sensibilities, and many of the other top stylists were most notable for their highly individual sounds, including John Abercrombie, the very popular Pat Metheny, Mike Stern, John Scofield (who brought in a country twang) and the highly original and versatile Bill Frisell. Bebop continued to develop in the hands of Jim Hall (an early influence on Pat Metheny), the underrated but explorative Lenny Breau and Ed Bickert. Joe Pass, the most prominent representative of the Charlie Christian school, found a major niche for himself by performing bebop both up tempo and unaccompanied, and Stanley Jordan with his tapping technique transformed his guitar into an orchestra of its own, often sounding like two or three players at once.

The jazz guitarist in the 1990s, unlike in some previous decades, does not have only one path to follow or one style to master as can be seen by the very different approaches of John Scofield, Stanley Jordan, Pat Metheny and Joe Pass. The key for the contemporary guitarist, as it is for all other instrumentalists, is to develop one's own individual style, mastering earlier styles so as to create new music for the future. That is the common legacy of Eddie Lang, Django Reinhardt, Charlie Christian, John McLaughlin and Wes Montgomery.

Scott Yanow
Jazz Columnist/Historian

LONNIE JOHNSON

Lonnie Johnson (1889-1970) was such a well-respected blues guitarist in the 1920s that he received opportunities to guest on recordings by the likes of Louis Armstrong, Duke Ellington, and on duets with his friend Eddie Lang. Throughout his lengthy career, Johnson mostly stuck to the blues, using his guitar to accompany his own vocals and occasionally take a solo, but it was clear from the start that, had he wanted to, he could have been a superior jazz musician, too.

Lonnie Johnson had the distinct accomplishment of being a major influence on both jazz and blues guitarists. Eddie Lang, the pacesetter in jazz of the late 1920s, considered Johnson to be his favorite guitarist, while few blues men of the 1930s (and even, in more recent times, B.B. King) were not affected by his subtle but passionate single-note run.

"Boogie-Woogie Blues" is a simple rhythm pattern included to represent not just Johnson but the many other blues guitarists from the 1920s who were generally more advanced than their jazz counterparts. This basic boogie rhythm shows how using just two lead notes can create a powerful mood. One can easily imagine Johnson and his contemporaries improvising single-note lines over the top.

BOOGIE WOOGIE BLUES

Med Tempo

Jimmy Stewart

EDDIE LANG

Eddie Lang (1902-1933) towered over all other jazz guitarists during his lifetime. Closely associated with Joe Venuti, the top jazz violinist of the era, Lang was in great demand as a studio guitarist, in addition to appearing in a wide variety of jazz settings. Only his early death from a botched tonsillectomy kept him from being a major force during the swing era.

In contrast to the monotonous chopping of most banjoists of the day, Lang's ensemble guitar sparkled with passing tones, chromatic sequences, whole-tone figures and single-string fills. His advanced chords were very sophisticated harmonically and were often quite impressionistic, making liberal use of advanced ninths and diminished chords. More than any other musician, he was most responsible for the guitar replacing the banjo in jazz and popular music.

"Pickin' My Way Home," named after his duet with Carl Kress, actually starts off with a quote from the other Lang-Kress duet *"Feeling My Way."* One can hear in the chord voicing echoes of the advanced Lang style which sounded a decade ahead of his fellow guitarists.

PICKIN' MY WAY HOME

Freely   **without measure**

Jimmy Stewart

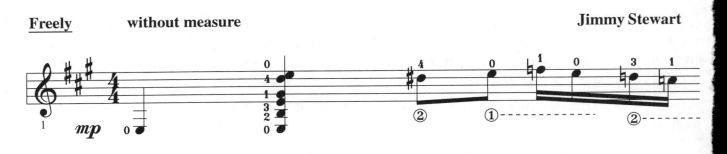

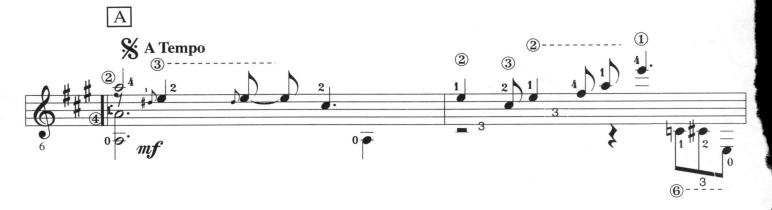

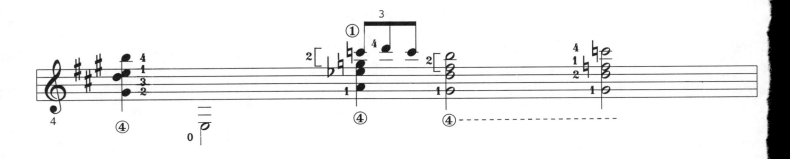

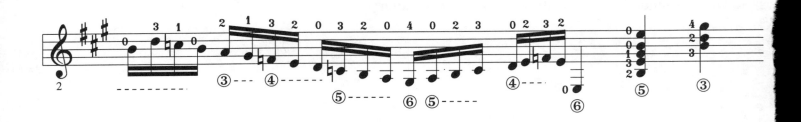

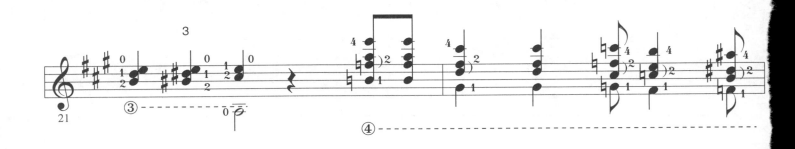

D.S. al Coda

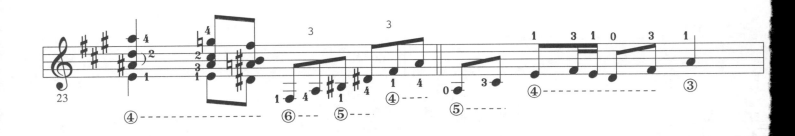

CARL KRESS

Of all of Eddie Lang's followers, Carl Kress (1907-1965) was one of the few to actually extend his harmonies and advanced chords. Lang himself recognized this in their two recorded duets; Eddie stuck mostly to single-note lines while the younger guitarist provided the chords. Kress, who first came to prominence in the late 1920s playing with Red Nichols and the Dorsey Brothers, helped to fill the gap (along with Dick McDonough and George Van Eps) after Lang's premature demise. Although his work in the studios kept him from ever achieving the fame he deserved, the duo that he formed with guitarist George Barnes in the early 1960s resulted in some of his finest recordings and some recognition late in his life.

As can be heard on the well-titled *"Miniature Orchestra,"* Carl Kress's voicings always had something going on inside of each chord. The harmony, bass lines and chords fit together so logically that his music sounds complete by itself.

MINIATURE ORCHESTRA

Jimmy Stewart

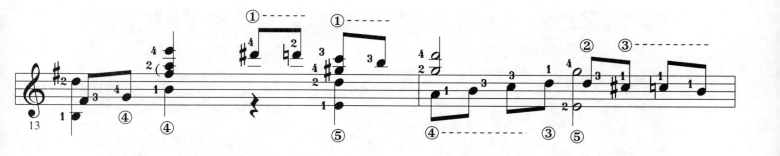

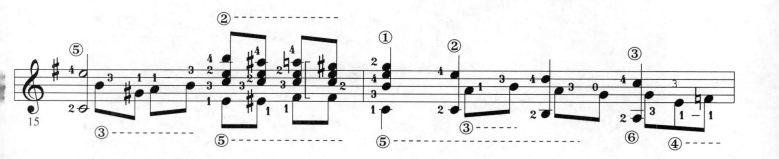

Artist	**Location**	**Photographer**
Jimmy Stewart	Birmingham Jam – 1991	Marilyn Greely
	Being inducted into the Jazz Hall Of Fame	
	Birmingham, Alabama	

DJANGO REINHARDT

Django Reinhardt (1910-1953) has always occupied a unique place in jazz history. Born to a gypsy family, Reinhardt, although essentially illiterate and handicapped in his left hand due to a fire, was the first great jazz guitar virtuoso. His stunning horn-like lines, combined with the influences of the French cabaret tradition and gypsy music, resulted in a totally personal style. He came to fame with the influences of the Hot Club of France, a group comprised of three acoustic guitars, violinist Stephane Grappelli and string bass. Django's strong rhythmic drive and powerful solos resulted in his becoming the first influential European jazz musician. In later years Django effectively switched to electric guitar and added the influence of bebop to his style, but he remains most famous for his earlier acoustic recordings.

A totally natural musician, Django's style was so personal and unusual that it took a while for him to become a strong influence. As can be seen on *"Django Gypsy,"* every bar he played had some surprising twists that were both logical and unexpected.

DJANGO GYPSY

Jimmy Stewart

FREDDIE GREEN

During the swing era, the acoustic guitar was utilized in big bands as a purely rhythmic instrument, pushing the ensembles while stating the chords. This now nearly lost art reached its peak of creativity with Freddie Green (1911-1987), the long-time guitarist with Count Basie, and the versatile Allan Reuss (1915-), best known for his association with Benny Goodman.

It is very easy for a rhythm guitarist to become bored and merely to play the basic chords of a song in repetitive fashion. Masters like Green and Reuss voiced their chords almost like a saxophone section, accepting the challenge to keep their parts musically interesting and inspiring to the soloists. "*Swing It,*" a tribute to these underrated masters, would sound perfect backing a lead voice, but at the same time says something musically by itself.

SWING IT

Jimmy Stewart

Med Groove

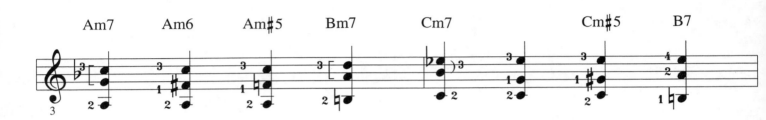

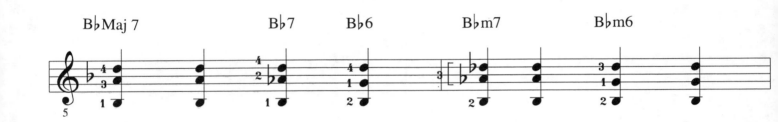

CHARLIE CHRISTIAN

Of all of the jazz guitarists, none had as strong an influence on future generations as Charlie Christian (1916-1942). The first significant electric guitarist, Christian used the guitar primarily as a solo instrument, taking inventive single-note lines that were as advanced as Lester Young's and looked towards bebop. He spent most of his short career as the well-featured guitarist with the Benny Goodman Sextet before his early death from tuberculosis.

Many of Charlie Christian's "licks" became the standard vocabulary of virtually all jazz guitarists. Some of his more famous ones can be heard in *Blues For Charlie.* His long swinging lines, advanced intervals and strong rhythmic ideas had a logic all their own. Even 20 years after his death, Wes Montgomery would state that Christian was his favorite guitarist.

BLUES FOR CHARLIE

Jimmy Stewart

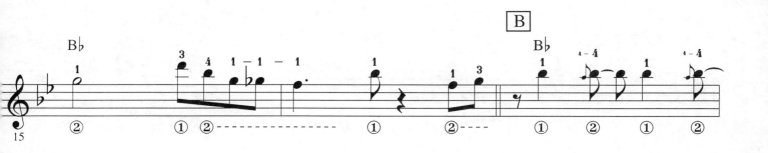

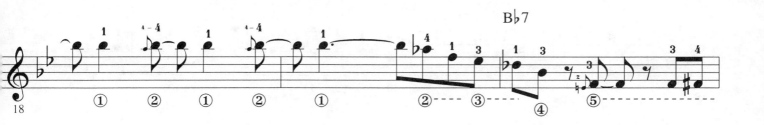

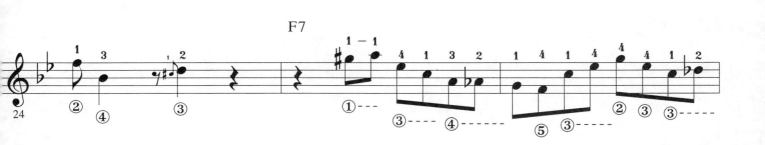

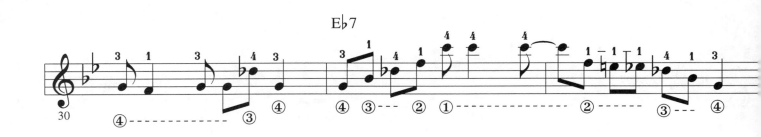

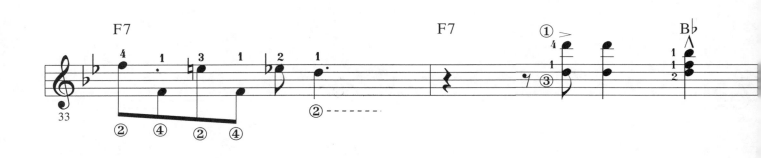

T-BONE WALKER

It could be stated without much exaggeration that T-Bone Walker (1910-1975) was the Charlie Christian of the blues world. An early associate of Christian (they both influenced each other), T-Bone was one of the first important electric guitarists to specialize in the blues. During his long career, Walker became best known for his composition *"Stormy Monday,"* but it is as a fluid jazz-oriented guitarist that he is most important.

Unlike the more primitive blues artists, Walker was sophisticated enough to create scales of his own from which to improvise, and did not feel limited to playing only "blue" notes in specific spots. *"Urban Blues"* is a good example of the freedom that his impressive technique gave him to express himself within the context of the blues.

URBAN BLUES

Jimmy Stewart

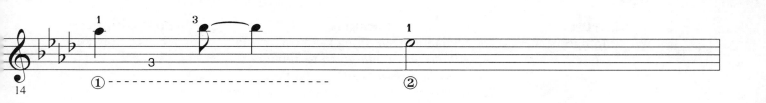

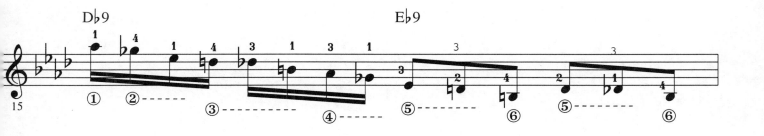

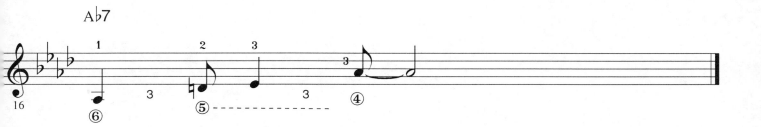

Artist	**Location**	**Photographer**
Wes Montgomery	El Madador – San Francisco, California	Charles Stewart
	Photo taken and given to Jimmy	
	while he was working on the	
	Wes Montgomery Jazz Guitar Method *book*	

STUDIO PLAYERS

Guitarists have been employed in the studios ever since the 1920s, including such important musicians as Eddie Lang, Carl Kress, George M. Smith, George Barnes and Les Paul among others. By the 1950s many of the top jazz guitarists found employment in the prosperous studio field and were in great demand to play for soundtracks. The influence of Andres Segovia on guitarists, particularly the studio players, is represented by this rendition of the *"Rachmaninoff Prelude."* This particular piano piece almost sounds as if it were originally written for the guitar, and it is a particular challenge to play with a pick.

RACHMANINOFF PRELUDE

Jimmy Stewart

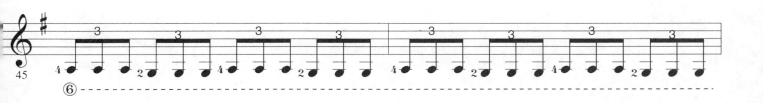

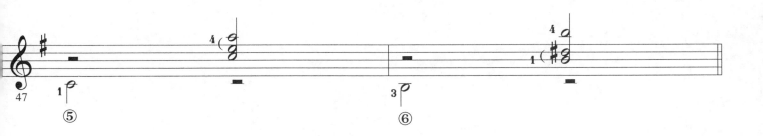

D. S. al Coda

33

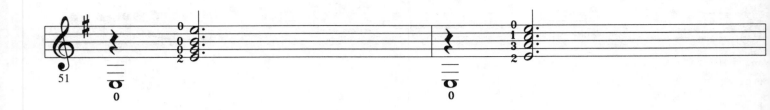

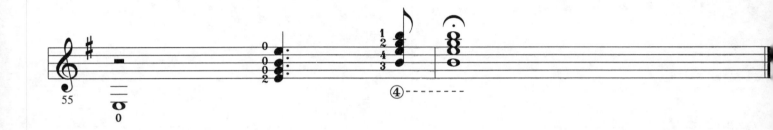

JOHNNY SMITH

While the electric guitar had made the use of its acoustic counterpart a rarity in jazz by the 1950s, a few artists helped to keep the unamplified guitar alive, especially the Spanish classical player Laurindo Almeida (1917-). Almeida was featured with Stan Kenton's Orchestra, and the very popular Johnny Smith (1922-), who had a major hit with his recording of *"Moonlight In Vermont"* in 1952.

Smith, who was an influential studio guitarist in the 1950s, could be called the Aaron Copeland of the guitar. He has a beautiful acoustic sound, perfect articulation and a chordal style notable both for its surface simplicity and deep sophistication since he has a way of really bringing out the beauty to be found in simple melodies. *"Black Is The Color Of My True Love's Hair"* is an example of how he might treat the traditional folk song.

BLACK IS THE COLOR

Jimmy Stewart

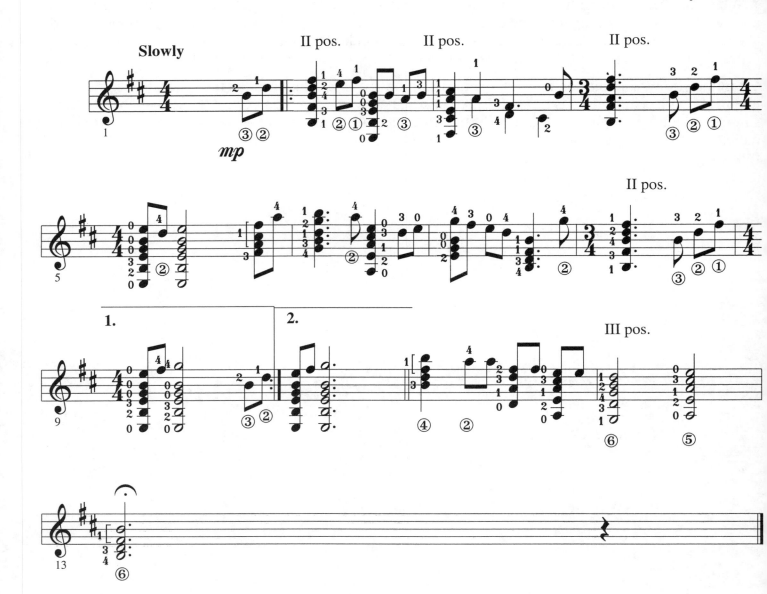

BARNEY KESSEL

Of all of the guitarists to emerge shortly after Charlie Christian's death, Barney Kessel (1923-) at first came closest to capturing Christian's sound and style. By the 1950s Kessel had developed his own approach, spending a year with the Oscar Peterson Trio and then recording a series of impressive albums. Through the decades he has remained one of the top bop-oriented guitarists, updating the innovations of Charlie Christian and transferring many of Charlie Parker's ideas, along with his own, to the guitar.

Although known for his single-note lines, Kessel also developed his own chord voicings. *"Barney's Tune,"* which emphasizes the latter, features the style that Kessel used in the late 1950s when he was a consistent "poll winner."

BARNEY'S TUNE

Med Groove

Jimmy Stewart

D. S. al Coda

JIMMY RANEY

Jimmy Raney (1927-) first came to fame with Woody Herman, Artie Shaw and particularly in a heated version of the Stan Getz Quintet, where his cool-toned guitar echoed Getz's sound. Raney has long been known as one of the most consistent of all jazzmen, a player who can always be counted on to swing passionately at a low volume.

Noted for his original chord changes and delicate sound, Jimmy Raney always seems to be able to find the prettiest note to play. *"A Little Raney"* is a waltz dedicated to this underrated master.

A LITTLE RANEY

Jimmy Stewart

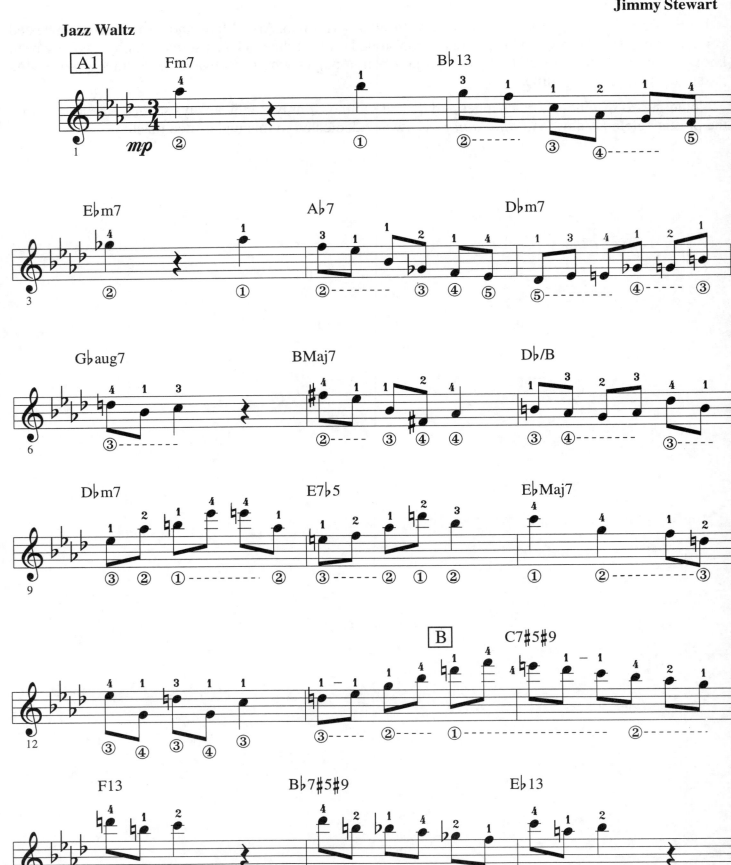

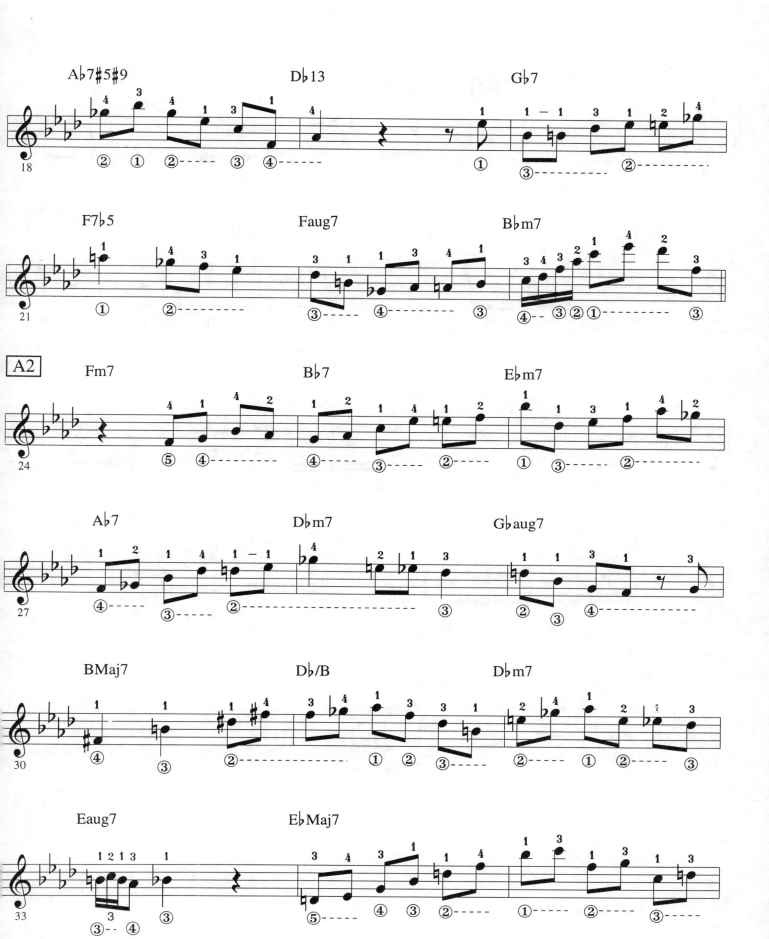

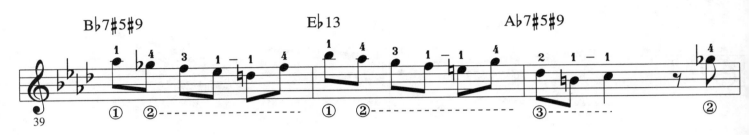

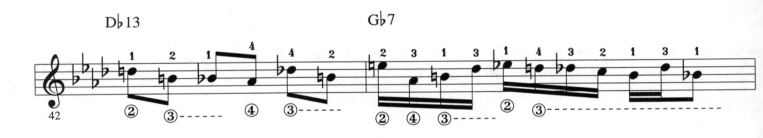

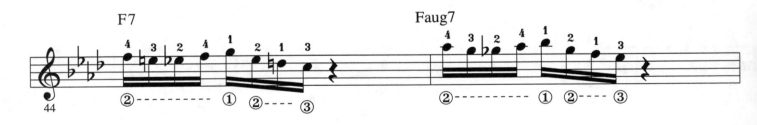

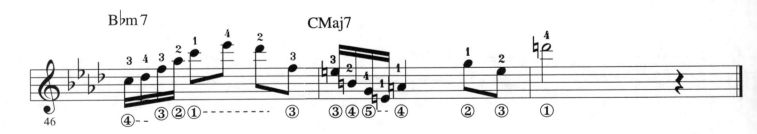

TAL FARLOW

In contrast to Jimmy Raney, and although both come from the same bebop tradition, Tal Farlow (1921-) is a monster. He first gained recognition as the key member of Red Norvo's vibes-guitar-bass trio and, despite several periods of semi-retirement, he remains one of the top guitarists around in the 1990s.

A very powerful but remarkably clean player who is capable of playing breathtaking, yet flawless, solos at rapid tempos, Farlow is blessed with huge hands and a surprisingly light touch. *"Gibson Man"* is a tribute to his hard-swinging style.

GIBSON MAN

Jimmy Stewart

Med Groove

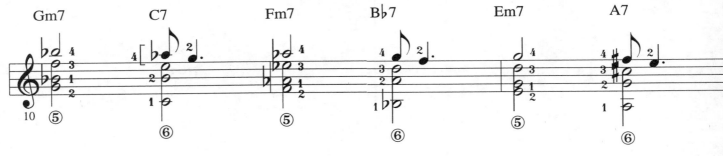

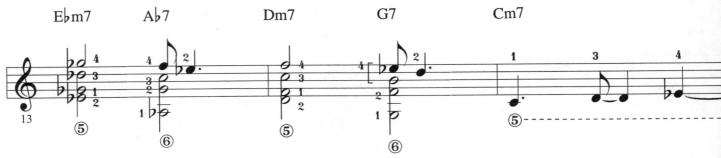

Ab13   G13   Cm11   B7#5#9

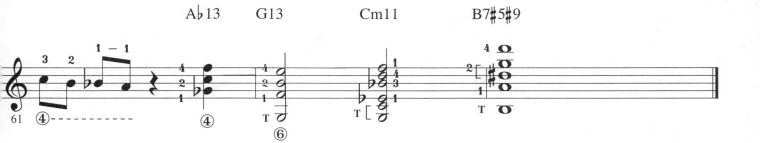

Artist	**Location**	**Photographer**
Les Paul and Jimmy Stewart	1993 – Los Angeles, California	Andy Brauer

WES MONTGOMERY

The most famous jazz guitarist of the 1960s, Wes Montgomery (1923-68) is rightly celebrated for his trademark octave, but his lyricism is sometimes overlooked. After touring with Lionel Hampton during 1948-50, Wes spent most of the next decade in obscurity playing in Indianapolis. When he emerged fully formed in 1959-60, he created a sensation in the jazz world with his stunning technique, his highly original melodic imagination and his refreshing ideas. A few years before his death, Montgomery and his record producers hit upon a very successful commercial formula, reducing his recordings to simplistic interpretations of pop melodies almost exclusively using his octave, but Wes was always a hard-swinging and creative improviser, as his live recordings attest.

The ballad *"Midnight Cool"* puts the focus on Wes Montgomery's pretty sound, unusual harmonies and Ellingtonish lyricism, tossing in a few octaves at its conclusion so one will not mistake him for anyone else!

MIDNIGHT COOL

Jimmy Stewart

53

GEORGE BENSON

    With Wes Montgomery's death in 1968, George Benson (1943-) stepped in to fill the void. Although his hit pop vocal records (starting with *This Masquerade*) have sometimes overshadowed his guitar playing. Benson brought the style of Charlie Christian into the 1960s and '70s. Benson added his virtuoso technique, a strong feel for the blues and developed the funkier side of his jazz, something that still makes him one of the most potentially exciting jazz guitarists of the 1990s.

    "Get Down" lives up to its title, emphasizing the funky riffs that Benson developed to play blues. Although one could imagine Charlie Christian performing this, Benson's personality makes his solos uniquely his own.

GET DOWN

Med Groove

Jimmy Stewart

Chorus 1

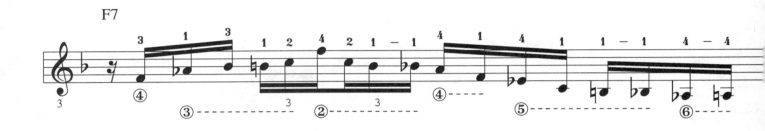

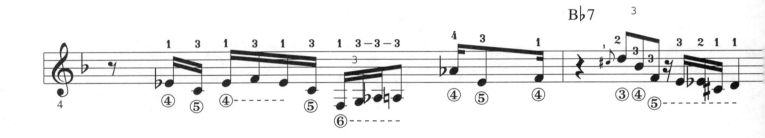

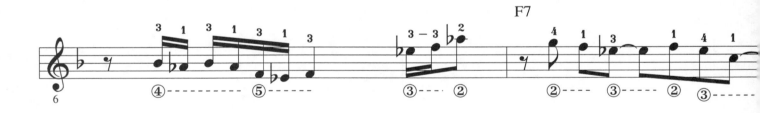

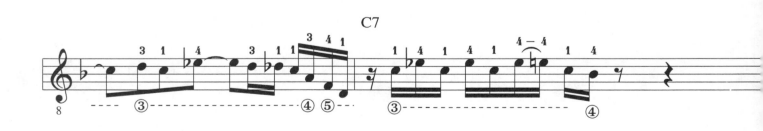

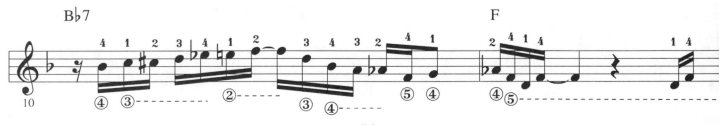

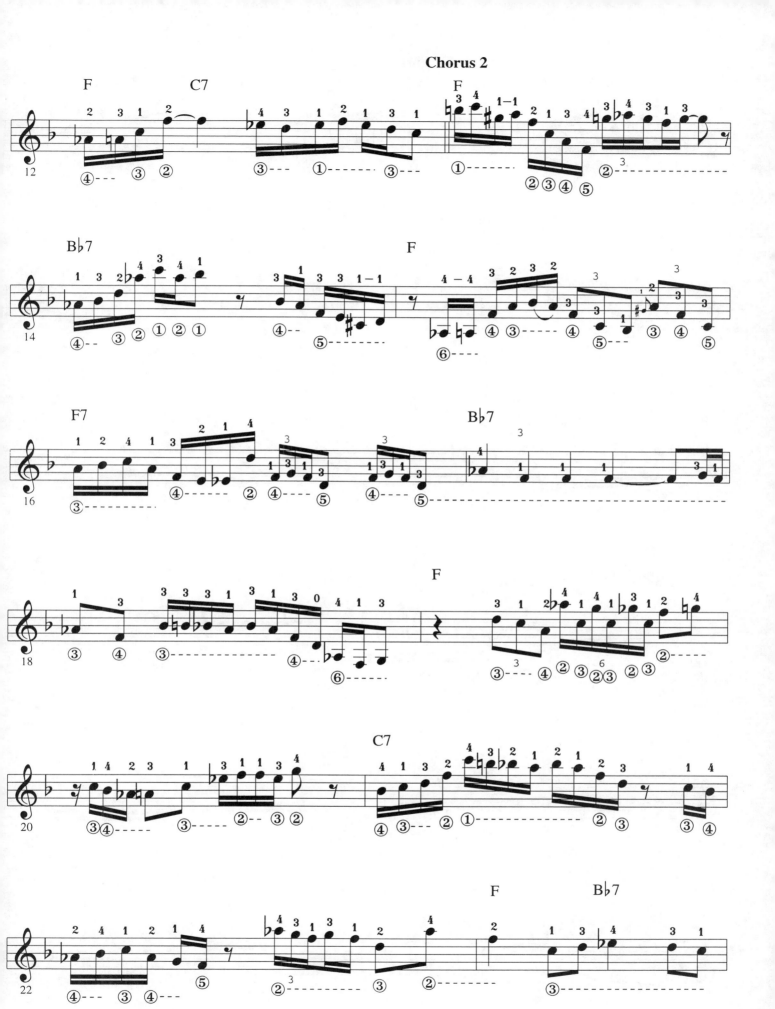

Chorus 3

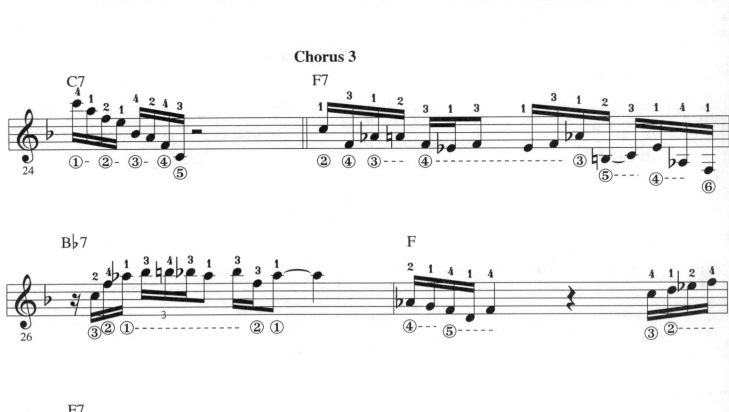

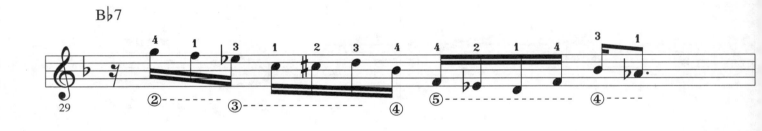

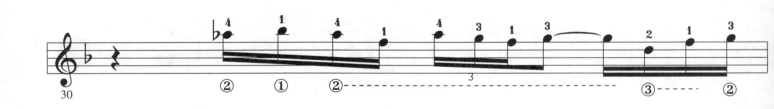

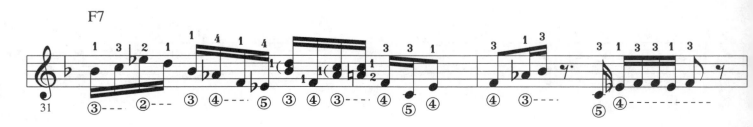

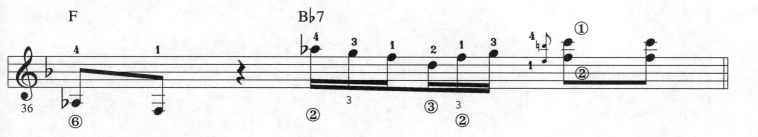

Cadenza

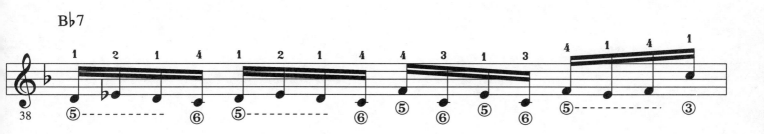

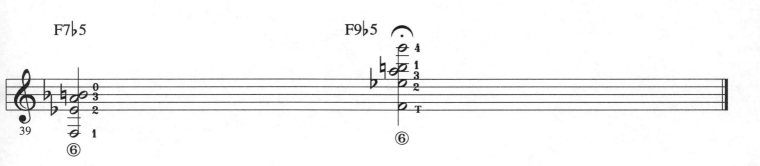

59

| **Artist** | **Location** | **Guitar** | **Photographer** |
| Jimmy Stewart and Gabor Szabo | Newport Jazz Festival – 1968 | Baldwin Classical | Charles Stewart |

JIM HALL

Of the veteran guitarists active in the 1990s, Jim Hall (1930-) is considered one of the most modern. After important stints with the Chico Hamilton Quintet and the Jimmy Giuffre Three in the mid-to-late 1950s, Hall performed frequently with Paul Desmond and Sonny Rollins in the 1960s. Hall has been a leader ever since.

The definitive West Coast jazz player, Jim Hall seems eternally modern. It would take hours to compose what he improvises in minutes, for he never plays the obvious and is a very compositional soloist. *"Samba For Mr. Hall"* demonstrates how he might come up with unexpected ideas to play on a melodic samba; none of his phrases are predictable.

SAMBA HALL

Jimmy Stewart

Jazz Samba

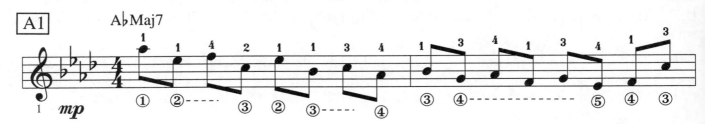

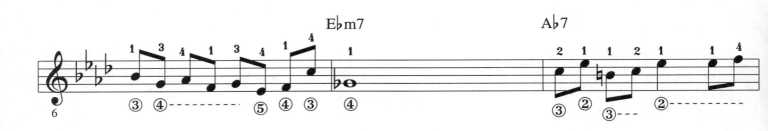

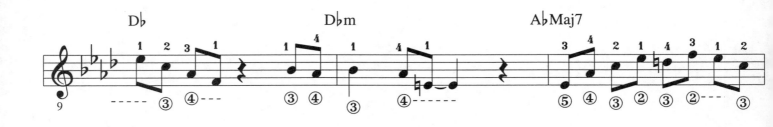

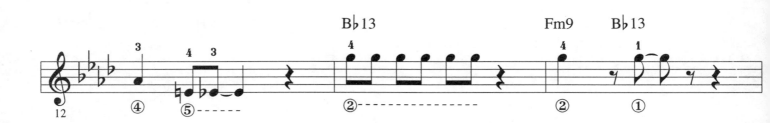

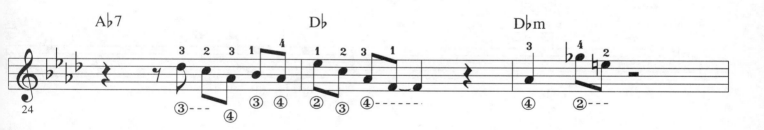

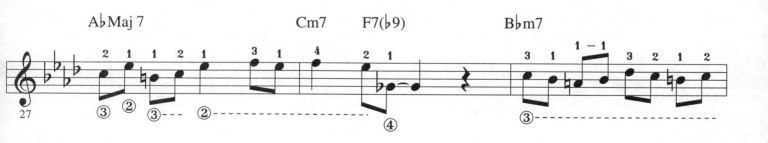

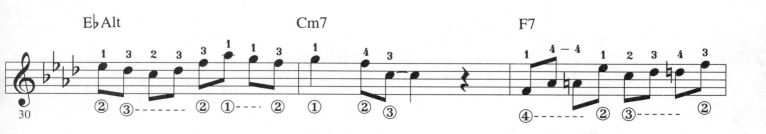

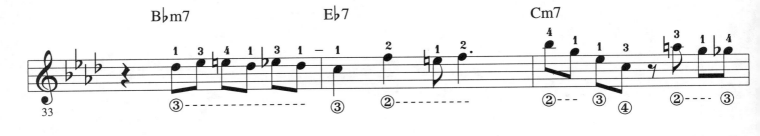

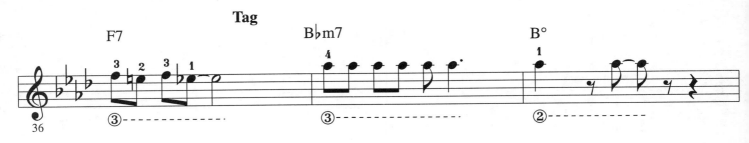

Tag

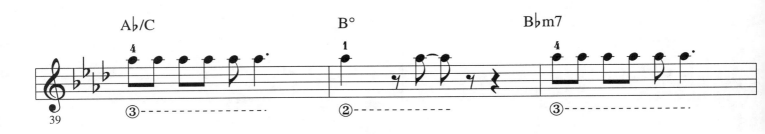

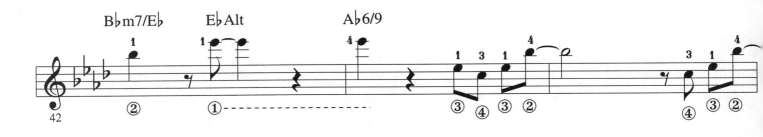

PAT MARTINO

A major transition figure between bop, the avant-garde and early fusion, Pat Martino (1944-), a predecessor of John McLaughlin and Pat Metheny, was himself influenced by Johnny Smith and Wes Montgomery. His outstanding technique, which allowed him to play very rapid lines, made him one of the most advanced of the bop-based guitarists. After several noteworthy recordings, in 1980 Martino suffered an aneurysm that caused him to lose part of his memory, including his ability to play music. It would be four years before he had retaught himself what he had previously known.

"Lines 1" pays tribute to Pat Martino's adventurous spirit and his highly individual style.

LINES 1

Jimmy Stewart

Med Groove

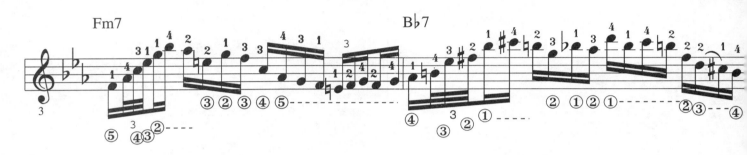

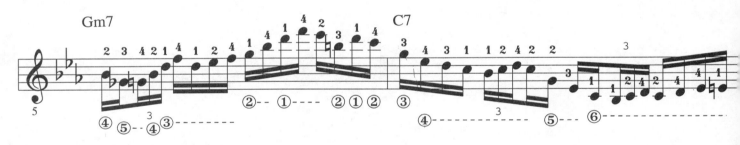

JOHN MCLAUGHLIN

John McLaughlin (1942-) had such a major success as the leader of the Mahavishnu Orchestra that he was initially categorized as a brilliant rock guitarist, but as it turned out, rock is only one part of this multi-faceted musician. McLaughlin, equally brilliant on both electric and acoustic guitars, has excelled in fusion (with Tony Williams' Lifetime), rock, World Music (including flamenco and, with the group Shakti, music from India) and more conventional jazz styles. Simply put, his virtuostic technique and totally open musical mind can tackle any style.

The complex *"Concertino"* at first does not seem like a logical outgrowth of earlier jazz stylists, but McLaughlin, like the speed king Al DiMeola and many of today's top younger players, has always been open to other influences outside of jazz. He has fulfilled some of the promise of Jimi Hendrix, the innovative rock guitarist who may very well have played jazz if it were not for his early death.

CONCERTINO

Jimmy Stewart

Solo Cadenza

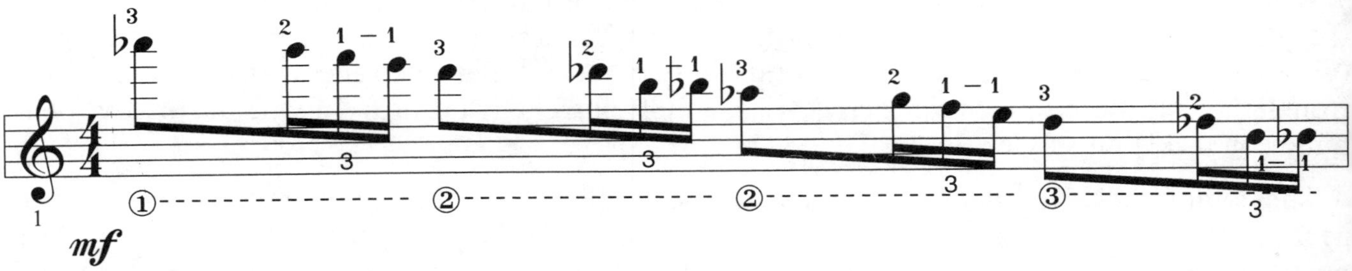

Maestoso

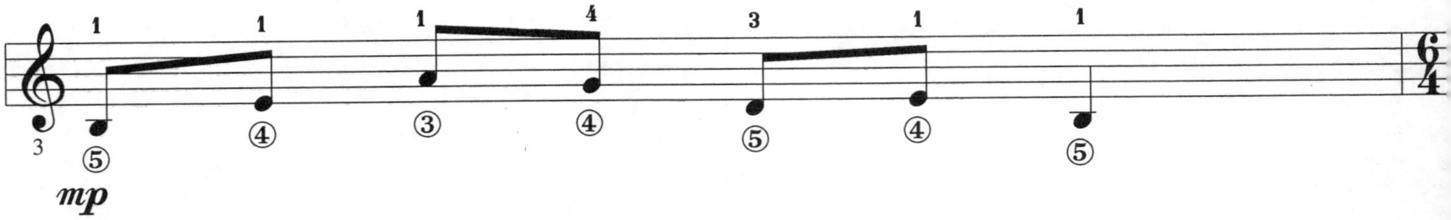

Con Moto

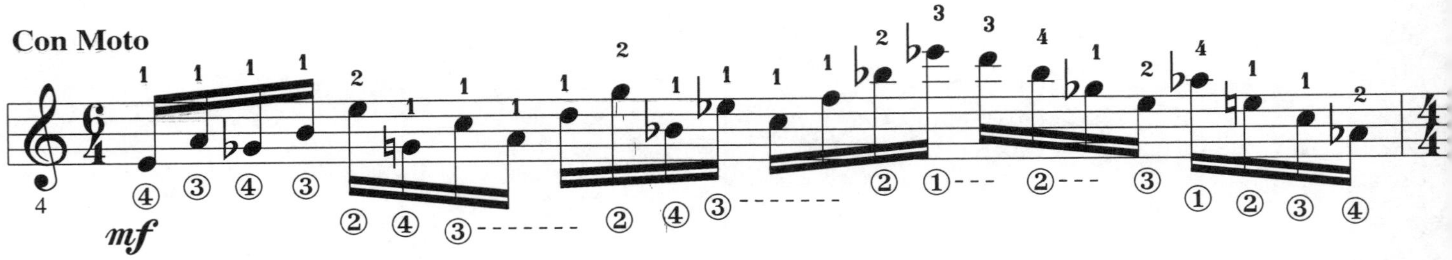

Cantabile

Misterioso

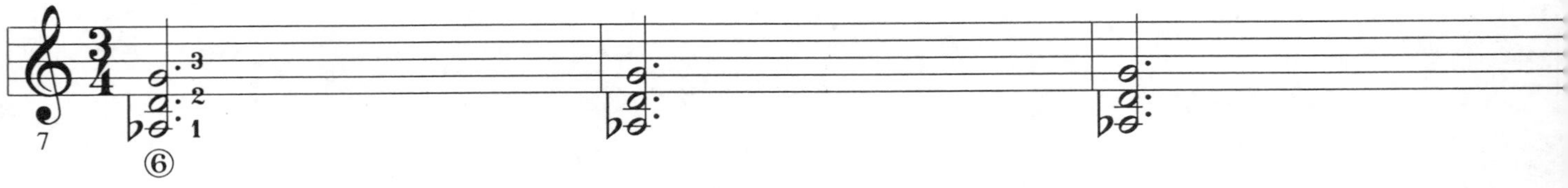

Con Fuoco

Espressivo

Misterioso

Agitato

Dolce

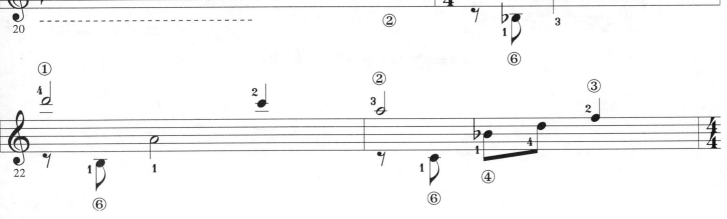

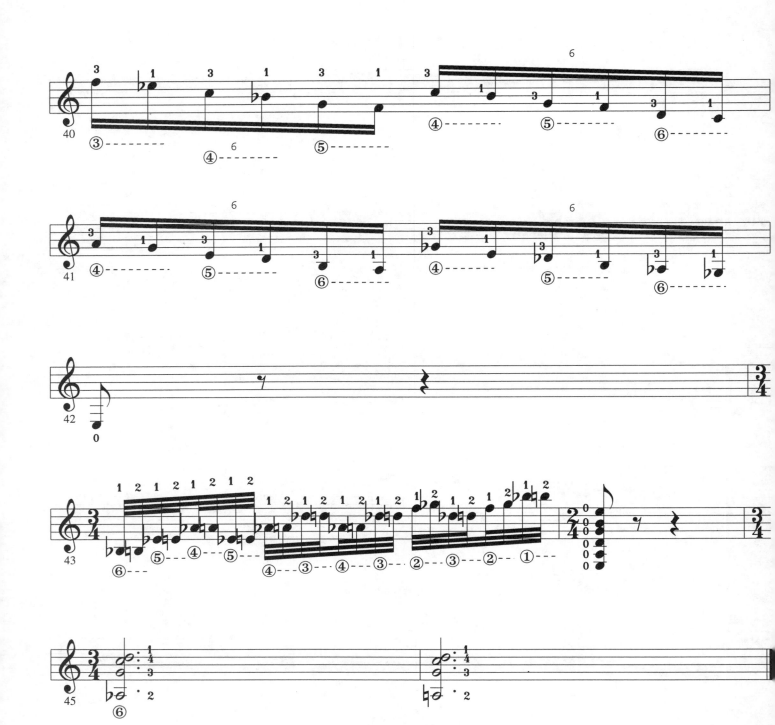

LENNY BREAU

Probably the least-known jazz guitarist represented in this book, Lenny Breau (1941-84) was one of the first to use the guitar as a sort of one-man band. By tuning the extra string of his seven-string guitar in the upper rather than lower register, this versatile player sought to make his guitar have the range and independence of a piano.

"Walkin" illustrates Lenny Breau's distinctive walking baseline and self-sufficiency over the chords of the standard *"Stella By Starlight."* It is little wonder that today he remains an underground legend among guitarists.

WALKIN'

Med Tempo

Jimmy Stewart

Artist
Jimmy Stewart

Location
Dick Grove Music Workshop – 1970s
Jimmy teaching one of his classes

Photographer
Buddy Childers

LARRY CARLTON

While the studio players of the 1950s were often as heavily influenced by classical music as by jazz, their counterparts two decades later were very much open to pop music's melodies, harmonies and rhythm. Larry Carlton (1948-) and Lee Ritenour (1952-) are perfect representatives of this new breed of guitarist, one quite familiar with the jazz tradition but also quite aware of the newer sounds being made in the pop music world. In addition to his own varied solo records, Larry Carlton was also a major asset on several albums by the Crusaders.

"Country Jam" features Carlton's sound and voicings in a poppish setting that also has the feel of country music. Whether it be blues, rock or jazz, Larry Carlton retains his strong personality no matter what the setting.

COUNTRY JAM

Jimmy Stewart

Country Jazz

78

| **Artist** | **Location** | **Guitar** | **Photographer** |
| Jimmy Stewart | Donte's Jazz Club – 1975
Los Angeles, California | Gibson 335 | Evan Wilcox |

JOE PASS

Although a respected guitarist by the early 1960s, it was not until he recorded his first solo album, *Virtuoso,* in 1973 that Joe Pass (1929-) began to amaze the jazz world.

His quick mind and masterful technique allowed him to play bop standards like *"Cherokee"* and *"How High The Moon"* unaccompanied; even with Pass's reliance on single-note lines, somehow one did not miss the other instruments. He remains a vital force today, bringing the Charlie Christian style into the 1990s.

"Joe's Soul-O" features Pass's distinctive style improvising over the chords of *"You Stepped Out of a Dream,"* somehow filling in all of the parts and demonstrating that the guitar really can be a complete bop combo by itself.

JOE'S SOUL-O

Jimmy Stewart

Med Tempo

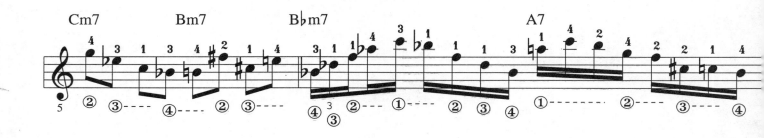

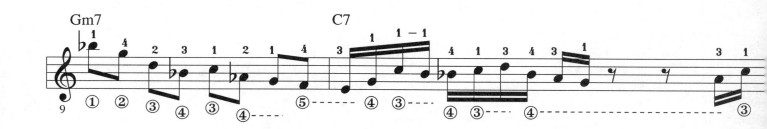

82

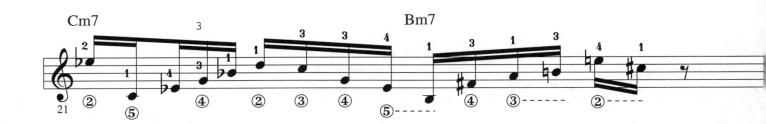

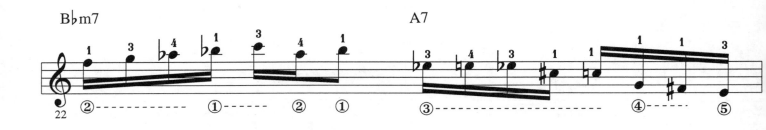

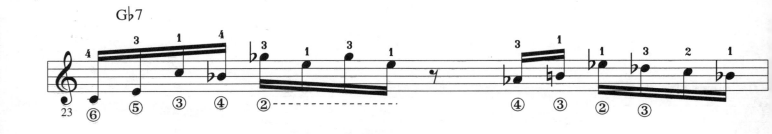

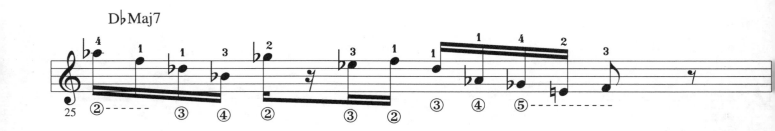

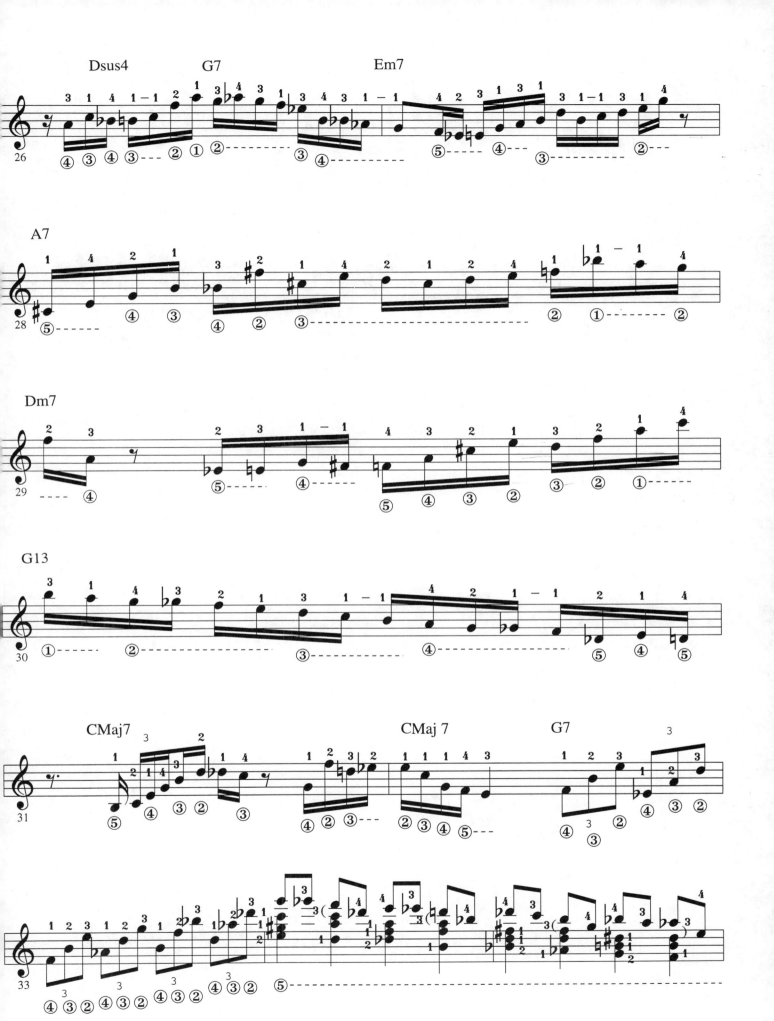

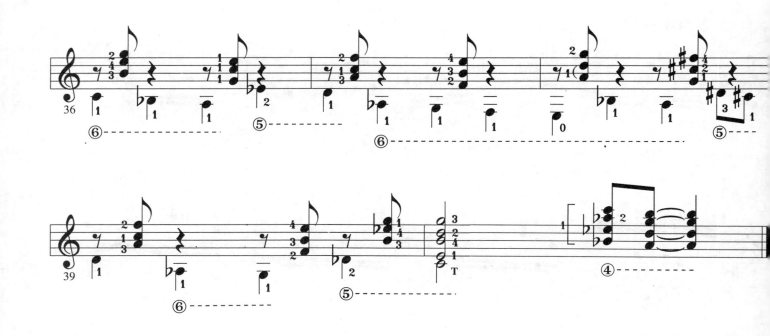

PAT METHENY

Unlike the Charlie Christian-oriented jazz players who tended to have similar sounds, a large part of Pat Metheny's (1954-) uniqueness has to do with his tone, a rather unique echoey sound. An advanced player whose versatility allows him to cross over between Jim Hall-style jazz to rock and folk music, Metheny's improvisations tend to be singable even at their most complex. The very popular Pat Metheny Group has brought many listeners more comfortable with pop music into jazz without compromising their ideals. Metheny has also recorded more conventional trio albums and collaborated on one session with his idol, altoist Ornette Coleman.

Typically, *"Night Hawk"* features Metheny's unique voice covering a lot of different moods, being consistently melodic and yet searching for new ideas.

NIGHT HAWK

Medium Jazz Samba

Jimmy Stewart

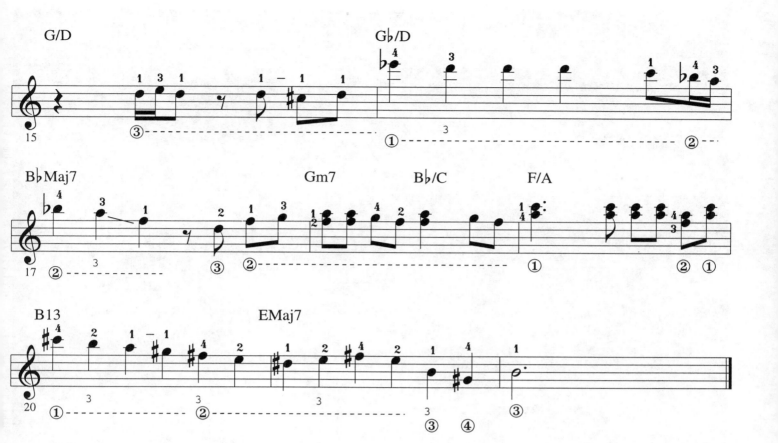

Artist	**Location**	**Photographer**
Jimmy Stewart	Wiltern Theatre – 1986	Motoo Ikami
	Guest artist with Carlos Santana	

STANLEY JORDAN

Although his influence is only now beginning to be felt, it is not an exaggeration to say that Stanley Jordan (1959-) has revolutionized the guitar. By mastering a remarkable tapping technique, Jordan frequently creates two or three separate melodic lines, playing his instrument like a piano with his two hands acting independently of each other and often sounding like two guitarists at once.

Many of Stanley Jordan's contemporaries have thus far avoided trying to incorporate this new technique, but it seems only a matter of time before it becomes a necessary part of any jazz guitarist's arsenal. *"Happy Fingers"* is a basic tune that can serve as an introduction to tapping for guitarists just beginning to learn this important new way of improvising.

Refer to Tips and Ideas for the description of Tapping Technique also known as the Touch System.

Note: + symbol = right-hand tap

HAPPY FINGERS

Med Groove

Jimmy Stewart

JOHN SCOFIELD

After a long period playing in a variety of jazz, rock and funk styles, including a few years with Miles Davis, John Scofield (1951-) has developed into one of the most important jazz guitarists of the 1990s. His unusual and very distinctive distorted sound is his trademark, while his style has become increasingly influenced by the open-minded approaches of fellow guitarist John Frisell, himself a major force, and Ornette Coleman. A bebopper of the 1990s, Scofield has remained open to the influences of free jazz and funk while playing in a pianoless quartet. *"Lines 2"* displays Scofield's style in a new composition but, as with Pat Metheny, capturing John Scofield's sound is almost as important as learning his style. As with all of the other guitarists represented in this book, John Scofield's originality and searching spirit is as impressive as his technique, and he succeeded in the main goal of any creative jazz musician: to find one's own sound.

LINES 2

Jimmy Stewart

Easy Swing

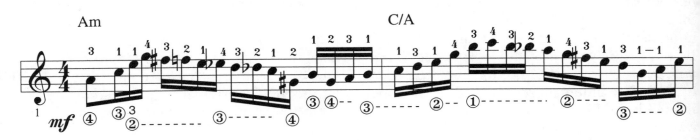

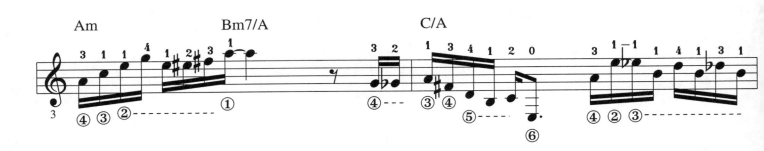

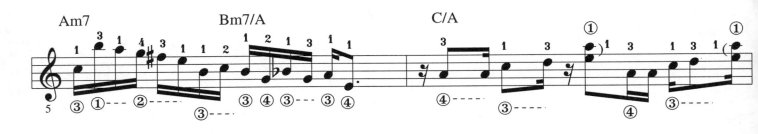

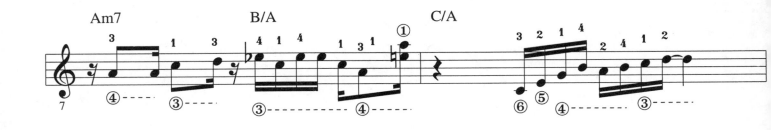

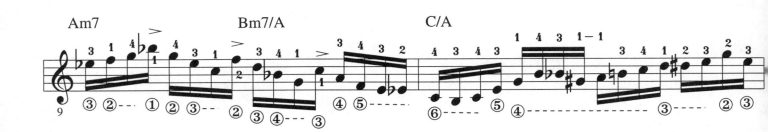

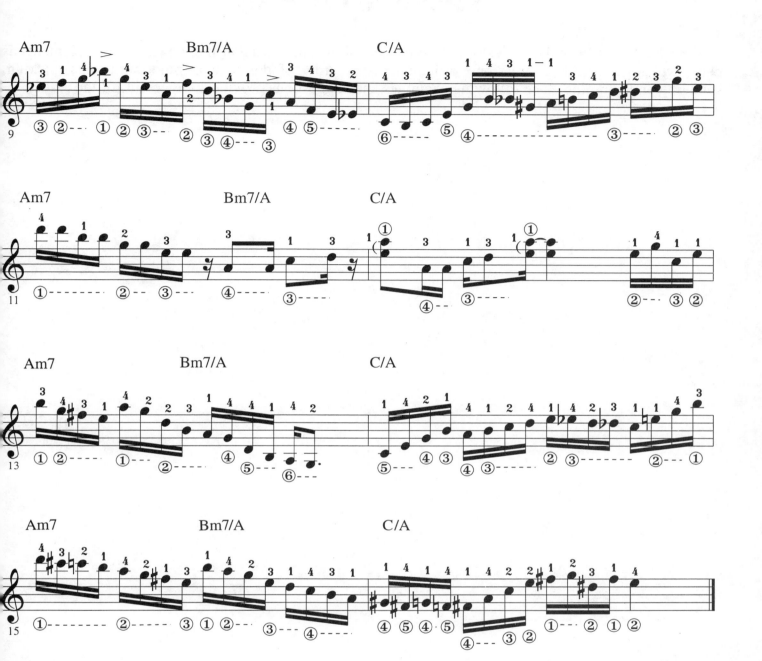

TIPS AND IDEAS

This chapter outlines the basics of jazz guitar technique and musicianship, covering such elements as chord voicings, chord progressions, articulation, the order of dominants, important scales, picking, swinging and comping. The following examples and suggestions provide a viewpoint for the player.

THE FINGERBOARD AND THE FIVE DISTINCT FINGERING PATTERNS

The *"five distinct fingering patterns"* when laid end to end cover the entire fingerboard from the lowest to the highest points in any key.

A full command of scales and variety of intervals are prerequisites to the command of each of the *"five distinct fingering patterns."* You should reach a point of visually seeing what you hear and be able to relate to one or more of the five basic fingering patterns.

When all of the five basic fingering patterns are telescoped into one position, you can play with ease in five different keys. In other words, two octaves and a third of chromatic tones are playable in one of the basic fingering patterns without moving the hand. A finger per fret is the general rule. The first finger is available to stretch down a fret and the little finger is available to stretch up a fret. Harmony does result from scales, and so do chord fingerings result from the *five distinct fingering patterns.* The *five distinct fingering patterns* can be visually related to the five basic chord forms; i.e., Cf, Af, Ef, and Df.*

Two basic rules for connecting the *five distinct fingering patterns*:

1 - Slide the fingers on the half-steps.

2 - Stretch with the little finger in ascending lines.

*The five basic chord forms are derived from the open-string six-note chords fingered in first position.

FINGERING 1

FINGERING 2

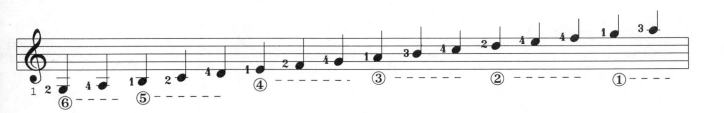

99

FINGERING 3

FINGERING 4

FINGERING 5

SLIDING ON THE HALF STEPS

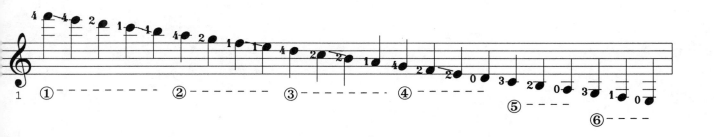

THE LEFT HAND
AND
THE FINGERBOARD

Position of the Thumb: Your knuckles should be almost parallel to the side of the neck. Fingers should be in an arched position until just the tips rest on the strings so that they work up and down in a hammer-like fashion, seating in between the frets. It is necessary to keep the fingers suspended over the fingerboard at all times. Do not let them stand up straight or curl under the fingerboard or wander in any fashion. The wrist must be kept straight at all times except when executing a very long stretch. This wrist posture should be comfortable and natural when used correctly. The attack should be a deliberate snap working to produce a good sound. The attack is the basic criterion for good sound and fluid technique.

LEFT HAND AND THE FINGERBOARD

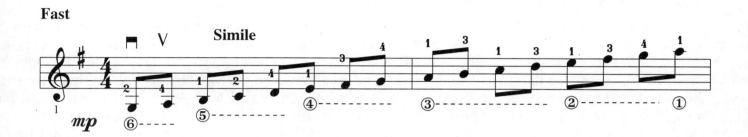

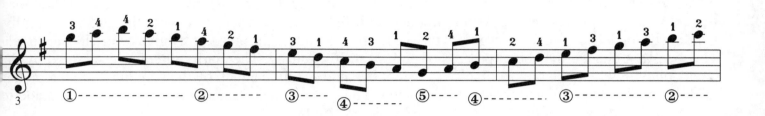

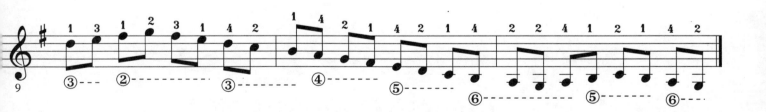

PICKING

Of all areas to be mastered, the technique of picking is the most personal and subtle, and is the identifying factor of primary importance in creating the individual's sound.

The picking motion is the end result of a series of coordinated muscular movements beginning with the shoulder and ending with the tip of the pick. This is a cantilever system, with muscles pulling fingers and the bone structure of the arm supporting the muscles. This system involves five separate areas: the shoulder, the elbow, the wrist, the thumb and index finger, and the tip of the pick. Movements that originate from the shoulder are large sweeping movements. The elbow motion is still a sweeping movement, but more controlled or confined. The wrist movement is a flicking type of motion. Rhythm playing comes from the shoulder, elbow, and wrist. Small circular scalpel movements are produced by the thumb and index finger single note playing.

The *attack* is achieved by the pressure point created by the thumb pushing the pick against the index finger. When the pick is held loosely it produces a different type of attack than with the pick held rigidly. Holding the pick in a rigid fashion gives you a rigid attack; holding the pick lightly gives you a looser attack. This does not change the actual process of pick contacting string. The clarity of sound is created by the precision with which the pick contacts the string; the quality of the attack by the way in which the pick is held. It should also be noted that in order to achieve a good attack, a conscious effort must be made to synchronize the action of the left hand with the picking motion.

BACK PICKING

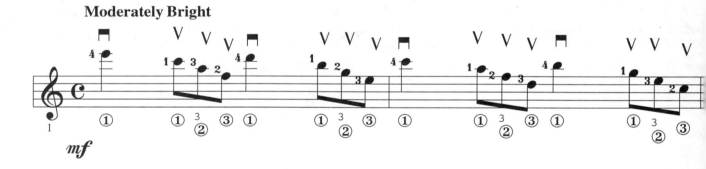

PICKING SEQUENCE

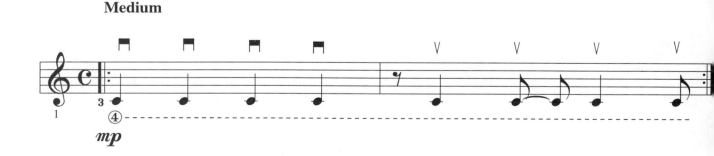

PICKING STUDIES

Picking studies will develop your left-and right-hand coordination.

CROSS PICKING

Slowly

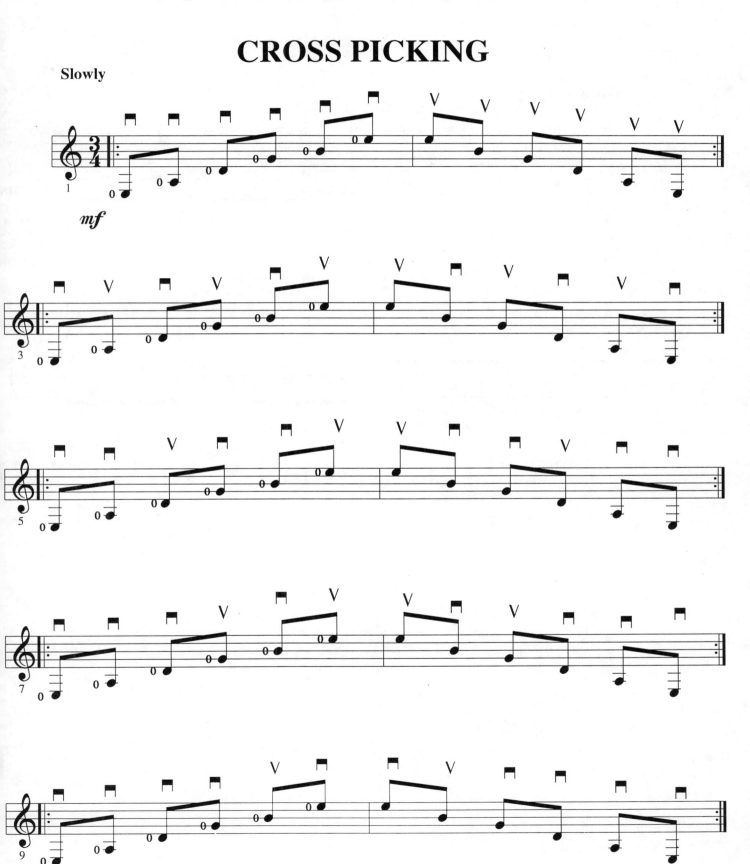

PICKING TRIPLETS

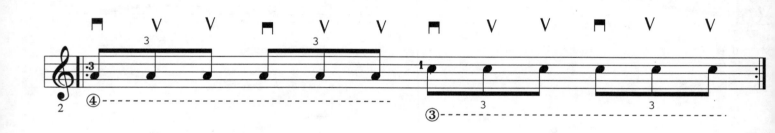

WARM-UP EXERCISES

The following warm-ups will get your fingers loose.

WARM-UP 1

Med To Fast

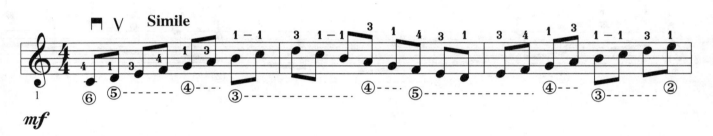

WARM-UP 2

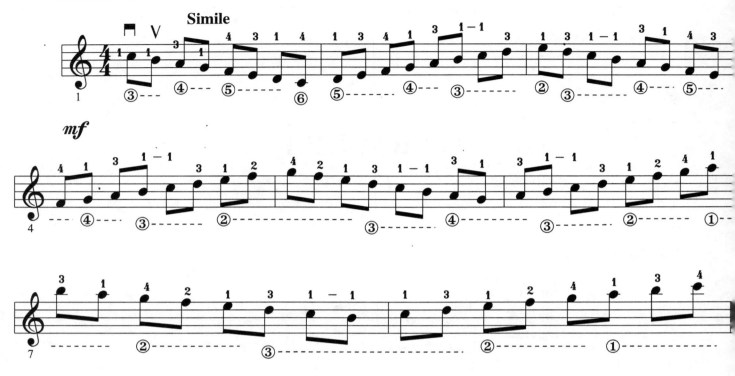

WARM-UP 3

WARM-UP 4

Med To Fast

WARM-UP 5

Med To Fast

WARM-UP 6

Med To Fast

WARM-UP 7

Med To Fast

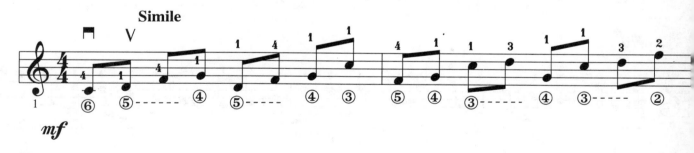

110

WARM-UP 8

Med To Fast

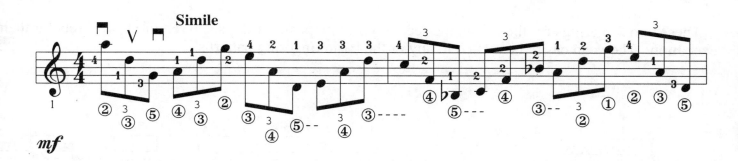

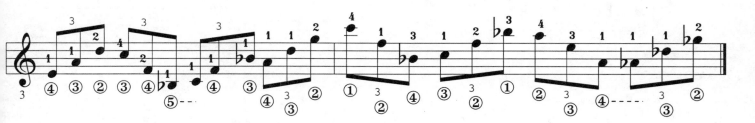

WARM-UP 9

Med To Fast

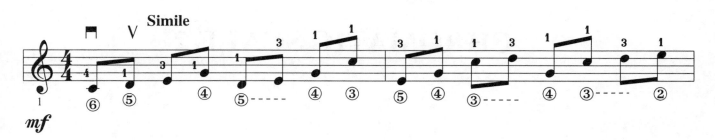

WARM-UP 10

Fast

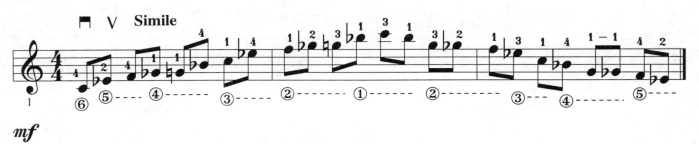

CHROMATIC SCALE 1

These two fingerings for the chromatic scale involve no position skips and require fewer frets for their execution. They can easily be related to any of the basic fingering patterns.

CHROMATIC SCALE 2

IMPORTANT JAZZ SCALES AND MODES

Thinking of scales and modes is much easier than thinking chords. The following examples typify the sound of jazz. This section describes the scale or mode and the chord it works well with. A scale is a set of notes with a particular arrangement of whole and half steps. Each scale or mode has a different sound and feel because of its unique arrangement of the intervals. Modes are arrangements of notes derived from the major minor and chromatic scales.

LYDIAN DOMINANT SCALE

2ND MODE MELODIC MINOR SCALE

ALTERED SCALE

C7Alt

BLUES SCALE

C7♯5   C   F   G

DIMINISHED HALF/WHOLE STEP SCALE

C7♭9

DIMINISHED WHOLE/HALF STEP SCALE

C°   E♭°   G♭°   A°

114

DORIAN MODE

Cm7

IN-SEN SCALE

F7#9   B13♭5

LOCRIAN #2 SCALE

Cm7♭5

LYDIAN SCALE

CMaj7♭5

LYDIAN AUGMENTED SCALE

CMaj7#5

MINOR PENTATONIC SCALE

C7   F7   C7#9

MINOR-MAJOR SCALE

Cm+7

MIXOLYDIAN MODE

C7   Csus

PENTATONIC SCALE

PHYGIAN MODE

WHOLE TONE SCALE

JAZZ ELEMENTS

These elements illustrate some of the distintive musical techniques used in jazz guitar.

ANTICIPATION

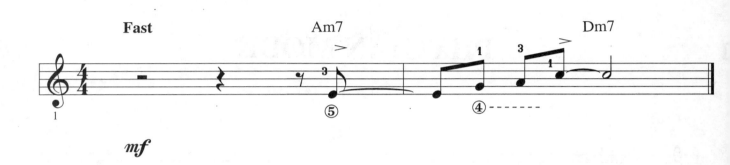

Anticipation

Anticipation adds to the swing feel of a tune. This is accomplished by playing any note that normally would be played on the beat, and pushing it ahead, making this note important, and off the down beat.

DOUBLE TIME FEEL

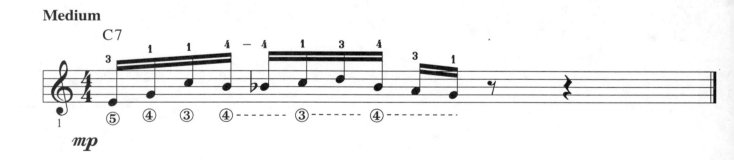

Double Time Feel

Many times a player will create a tension by doubling up notes over the established tempo.

FREE TONES

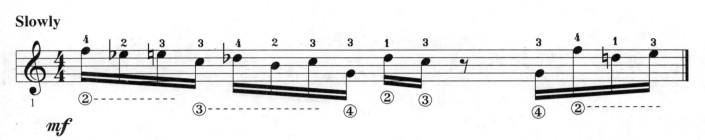

Free Tones

Free tones add color and character to a jazz phrase.

GHOST NOTE

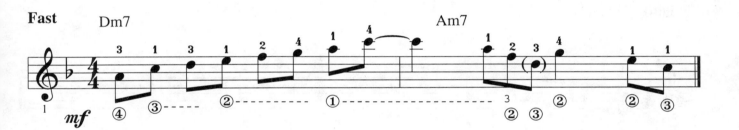

Ghost Notes

When the tempo is fast, these notes become more equal and interpreted as straight or regular eighth notes with an even feel to them. Sometimes a player will play a note not clearly defined, yet audible as a false image. These notes are called "ghost notes" and when written have parentheses around them.

IMPLIED CHORDS

Easy Swing

Implying Chords Not Played In The Background

The player may at times want to give the listener an ear trip by playing out of the key center, with the background staying in the key center.

MINOR 7TH PASSING CHORD

Brightly

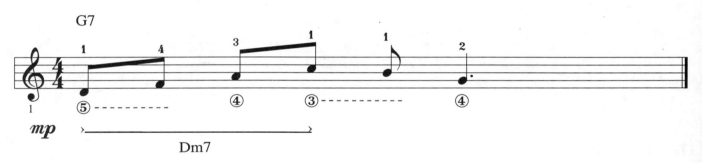

Minor Seventh Passing Chord

Instead of playing the notes of any given dominant seventh chords, the player may create a cooler sound by using the seventh chord in some form of an arpeggio.

THE FLATTENED FIFTH

Brightly

The Flattened Fifth

The flattened fifth tone became very fashionable during the '40s and is used in an unpredictable manner.

REPETITION

Medium

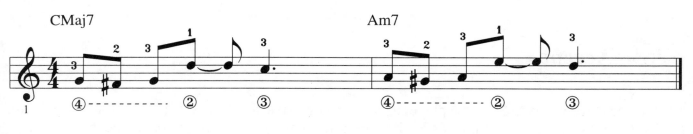

Repetition

A sequence is a recognizable series of notes repeating and starting again on new series of tones as a familiar repetition.

UP-BEAT ACCENT

Lightly & Brightly

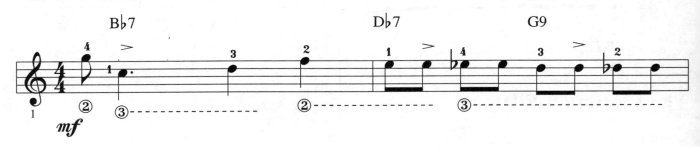

Up-Beat Accent

The "up-beat accent" is used by the player to create a new pulse for the listener, while the old one remains in the background. A special emphasis is given to notes that would normally be unaccented.

ARTICULATIONS

Articulations applied to the guitar create musical drama. Command of these touches are essential for producing good musical ideas.

GLISS

Medium

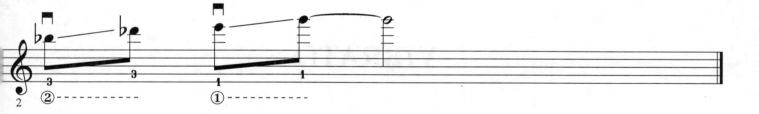

Gliss

The finger employed stops the first note as it is picked, then slides across the frets to the other note, pressing the string sufficiently to make the intermediate semitones sound.

GRACE NOTE

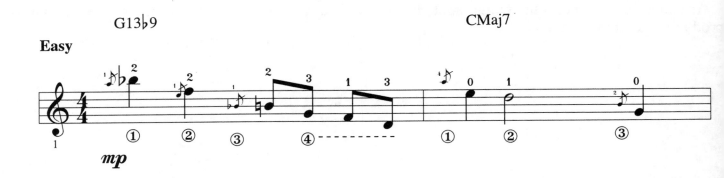

Grace Note

The grace note takes its time value from the note it embellishes. When the grace note is ascending, pick the grace note and, without moving the finger, stop it. Then let the proper finger fall on the following note to be sounded without picking; when descending, plant both fingers simultaneously, picking the grace note. Then lift the finger so the following note will sound.

VIBRATO

Vibrato

The vibrato is produced by a shaking motion of the left hand. The sound is a minute fluctuation of pitch in order to increase the emotional quality of the tone without resulting in a noticeable fluctuation of pitch.

ADJACENT STRING HAMMER

Brightly

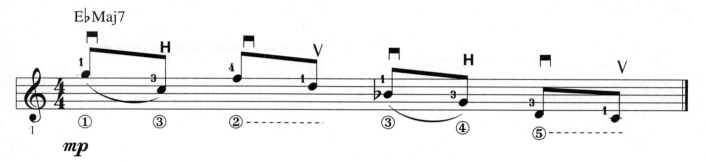

Adjacent String Hammering

To interpret this category of hammer-on, pick the first note; then let the proper finger fall energetically on the next note to be sounded.

FINGER ROLL

Medium Fast

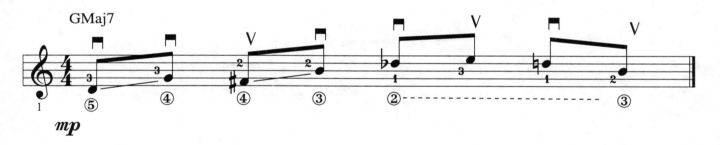

Finger Roll

The *finger roll* technique is another way of achieving a legato sound within a phrase. The first joint of any finger being used is snapped across the adjacent string when sounding it.

HAMMER ON

Easy Swing

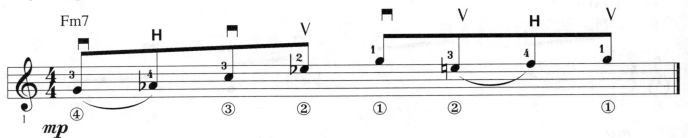

Hammer On

While the right hand picks the first note, the left hand can *hammer on*, executing two or more notes in a descending jazz line.

PULL-OFF

Almost Bright

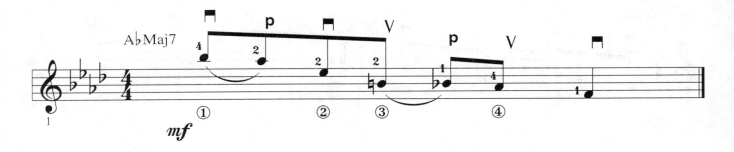

The Pull-Off

The pull-off is performed by picking the first note, then sounding the second note with the fretting finger being pulled in a downward notion across the fingerboard.

SLIDING ON HALF STEPS

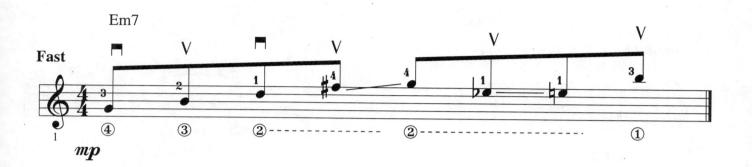

Sliding On Half Steps

Sliding on half steps adds to the flow of a musical phrase. Any finger can be used as long as the fretted notes appear on the same string and are a half step apart.

SMEAR OR STRING BEND

Smear Or String Bend

Essentially, the bend consists of stretching the guitar string against the fingerboard and raising the pitch of the note sounded.

SLIDE UP/SLIDE DOWN

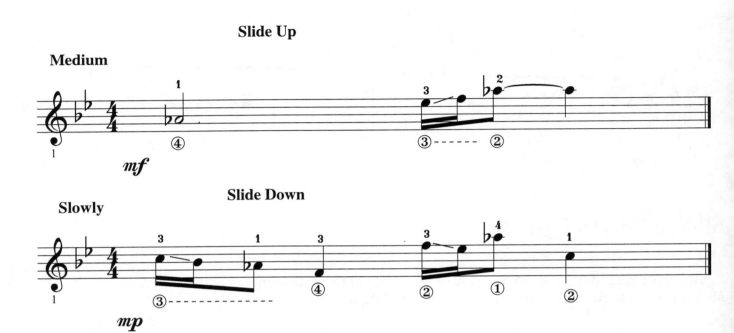

Slide Up/Slide Down

Finger pressure is maintained while moving from one note to another on the same string. It is actually one continuous sound.

THE ORDER OF DOMINANTS

The most common progression in jazz music is the order of dominants. The following are a few recognizable patterns.

DOM 7TH CHORD

130

MIN 7TH AND DOM 7TH

CHORD CHANGES

What separates jazz from other forms of music are its chordal harmonics. Major Blues, Minor Blues, and Modern Blues are rhythm changes that illustrate this concept.

MAJOR BLUES

Moderately with a beat

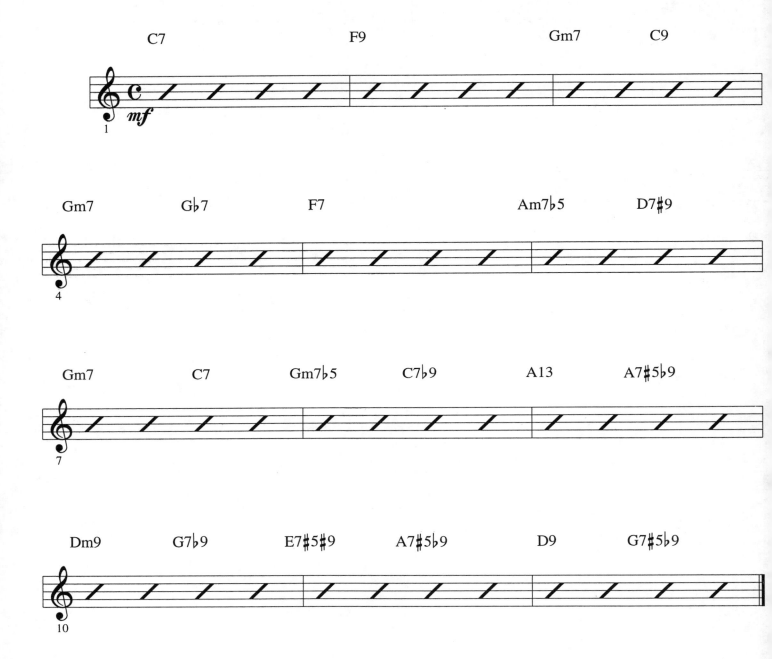

MINOR BLUES

Almost Bright

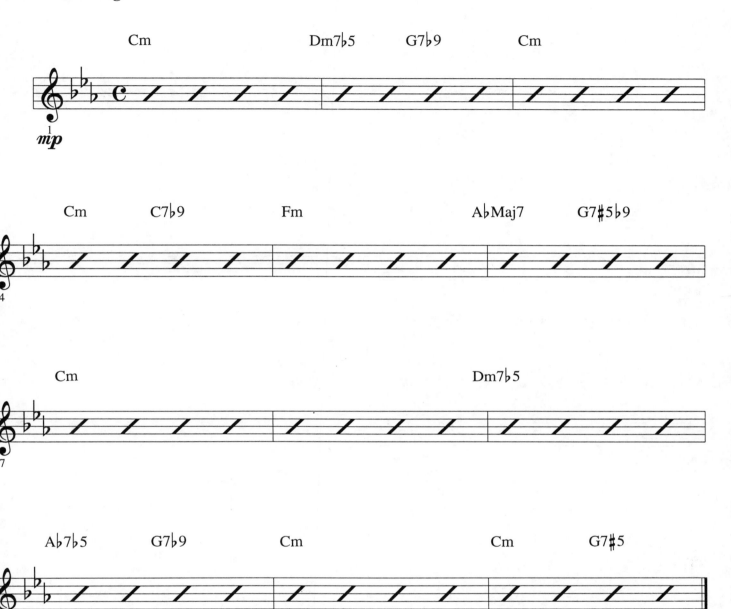

MODERN BLUES

Easy Swing

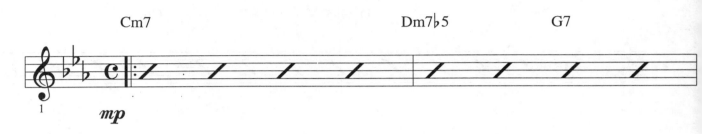

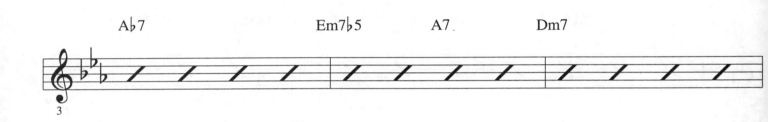

RHYTHM CHANGES

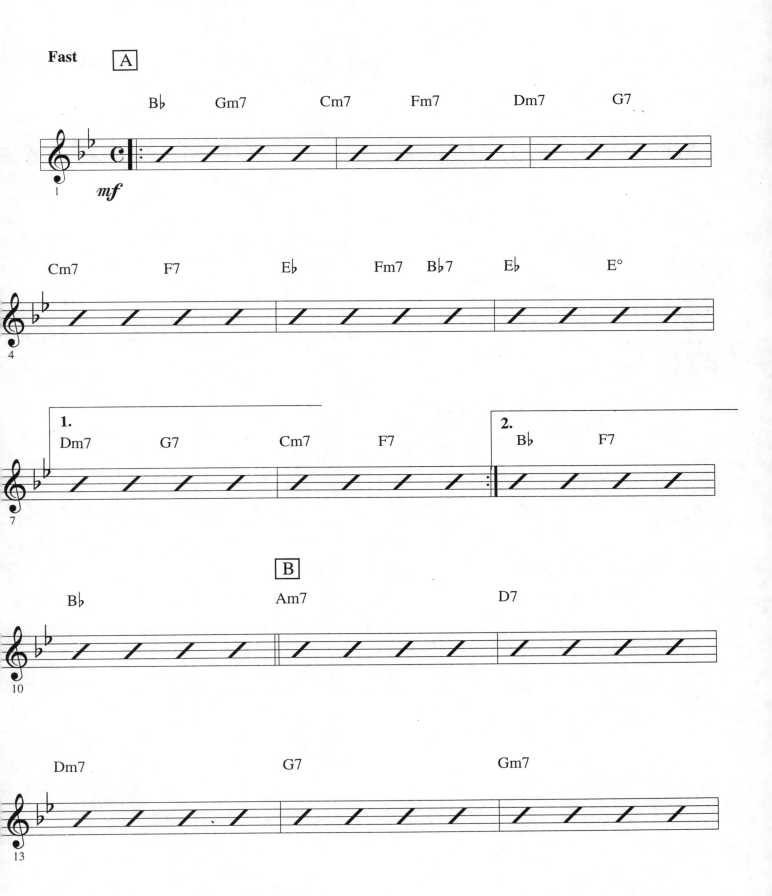

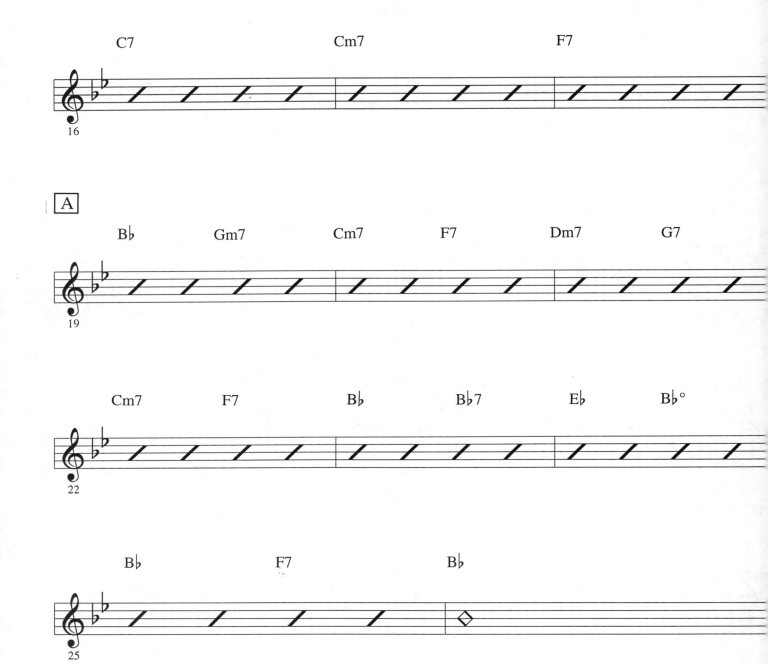

TURNAROUNDS

A turnaround is a short series of chords, occurring at the close within a section of a tune, which replaces an extended duration of the tonic chord. This deception surprises the listeners' ears by adding harmonic variety to the performance. All examples are relative to the key of C.

TURNAROUNDS

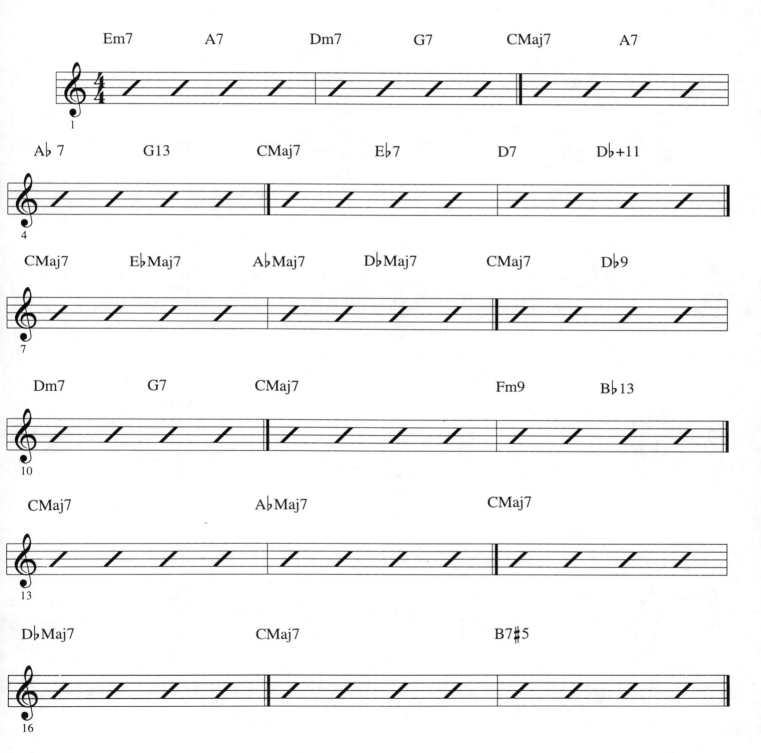

CHORD VOICINGS

There are unlimited chord voicings. Here are a few of my favorites, based on the common chord structures. All examples are relative to the key of C .

CHORD VOICINGS

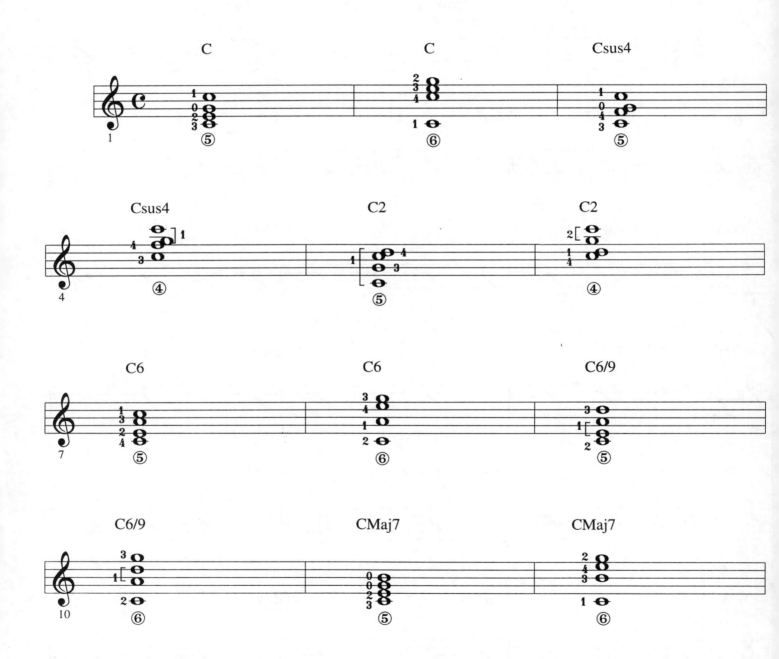

138

139

COMPING

A musician's term for the act of providing accompaniment is "comping." We shall highlight the important factors in accomplishing a good accompaniment in this chapter.

The most important factor in comping is the preservation of the feeling and mood which has already been established by the existing melody. It should be noted, however, that in some cases a cross-relationship of feeling and/or mood may be desirable.

In approaching the problem of accompaniment, first determine what the job calls for. Will the guitar be used as a percussive instrument, or will it be providing harmony, or both? What is the idiom or "bag" the accompaniment should be in? Is its purpose to act as a mirror or reflection of the melody, or to provide a blanket of sound over which everything else is happening? Will the guitar be used to reinforce the rhythmic feel of a piece, or is it to carry an accompaniment wherein its own melody will stand out by itself?

With the melody present, there are few guidelines that evolve from a fine accompaniment. When the melody has motion, the background sustains, and when the melody sustains the background moves. Composing a background to a melodic line is very similar to counterpoint and re-harmonization.

BACKGROUND MOVES

MELODY MOVES

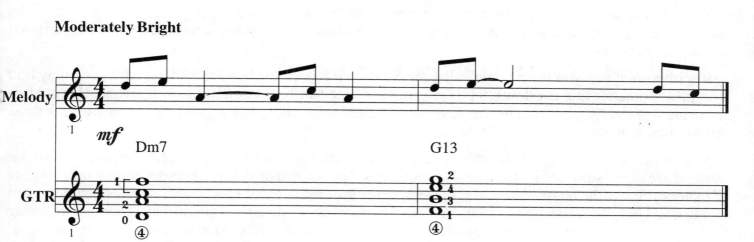

PUNCTUATING

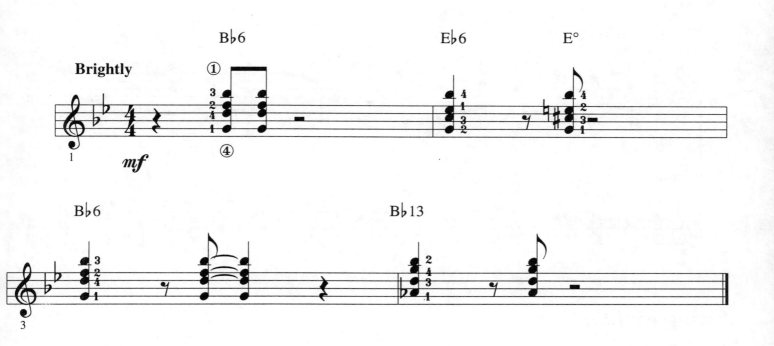

SWINGING

The missing factor that can't be notated is how to get the music to swing. Ironically, this is perhaps the most important element of jazz. It may not be an exaggeration to say that any series of notes will sound good as long as it swings.

It is important that you learn to play all three ways—on top, on the beat, and laying back. You may find it helpful to practice this at a slow tempo first, and then speed up the metronome as you get a feel for it. Most musicians generally play one of the three ways characteristically, but a good musician uses all three approaches, sometimes even within the same solo.

The reason notating swing is impossible is that the eighth notes are usually played somewhere between even (also called "straight eighths") and triplet values. The amount of swing varies depending on a number of factors. First is the tempo. The faster the tempo, the less of a triplet feel is possible. At fast tempos, even eighth notes may be the only possibility. The groove or feel of the music will also affect the amount of swing that you use. If you're playing in a group, the groove will be affected by what the other players are doing, and this may change from one section of the tune to another, or even from one phrase to another.

SWING EIGHTHS

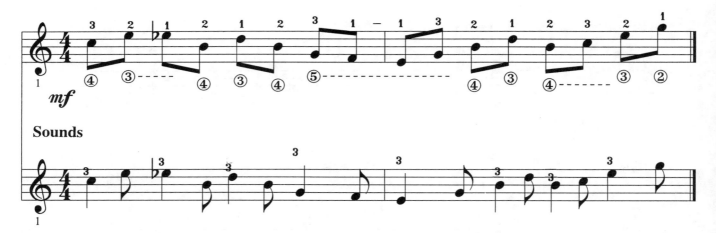

Swing Eighths

"Swing eighths" refers to the reinterpretation of the rhythm within a group of consecutive eighth notes. The sound has a loping, laid-back feel. This feel is applied to slow and medium tempos.

FLIP PICKING

Fast

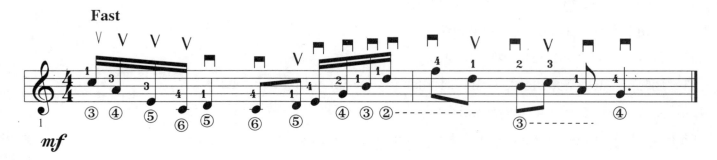

Medium Fast

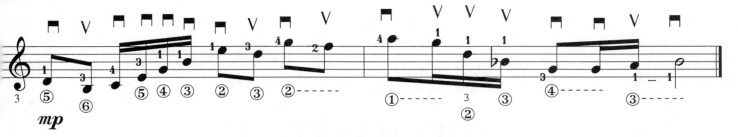

Flip Pick

Flip pick is consecutive up or down picking strokes across the strings in the same direction. This technique adds a unique flavor to the rhythmic feel.

TOUCH SYSTEM
THE TAPPING TECHNIQUE

Touch system in short means playing the guitar like a piano. Both hands are employed to reproduce musical tones much in the same fashion as you would play a piano. The first step is the development of the left hand. Place your fingers on the designated chord, then by pressing down firmly on the strings you will hear the chord. Develop a good firm press technique to sound the chords. The right hand is the real trick in *touch system.*

While the left hand is playing solid four-beat rhythms in the background, the right hand plays the melody. The coordination for right and left hand must be broken so both hands can play independently of one another. The 1st, 2nd and 3rd fingers of the right hand are employed mostly in the *touch system.* To sound melody notes, use only the *ball tip.* Do not peck at the string; strike firmly and hold down to the fingerboard. The string should always be struck between the frets.

TOUCH SYSTEM SET-UP

The Guitar - Use the finest pick-up available.

The Amplifier - Turn the volume up.

The Strings - Use only flat-wound strings.

The Bridge - Use adjustable string saddles to tune the guitar accurately.

Guitar Action - Set a very low action.

Pick-up Adjustment - Raise the pick-up and magnets close to the strings.

TOUCH SYSTEM

CONCLUSION

There are numerous other jazz guitarists not mentioned. Some guitarist not named individually include:

Teddy Bunn, who worked on 52nd Street in New York with his combo The Spirits of Rhythm; Al Casey of Fats Waller's Rhythm; Eddy Durham of the Jimmie Lunceford and Count Basie bands; Les Paul, who toured with Jazz At The Philharmonic, Sal Salvador with the Stan Kenton Orchestra; Carmen Mastern, studio guitarist in radio; Don Barbour, with the Four Freshmen; Dave Barbour, with Peggy Lee; Oscar Moore, Irving Ashby, and John Collins, with Nat King Cole; Herb Ellis, with the Oscar Peterson Trio; Tiny Grimes, tenor guitarist with Art Tatum; Mundell Lowe, West Coast soloist and arranger; Dick Garcia, Eddie Duran, and Toots Thielmans, who at various times played with George Shearing; Dennis Budimer and John Pizzarelli, Allen Hanlon, Barry Galbraith, Tony Mottola, and Al Viola, in the New York studio scene; Billy Bauer, with Lennie Tristano; and Jimmy Wyble, who played with Red Norvo and Benny Goodman; Soonzer Quin for his work with the Paul Whiteman Orchestra; Freddie Green, the blood and bones of the Count Basie Orchestra; four-string tenor guitarist Eddie Condon, founder of the Chicago School of Jazz; Oscar Aleman for his work with singer Josephine Baker; Freddie Guy with the Duke Ellington Band and Al Norris with Jimmie Lunceford; Al Hendrickson with Artie Shaw, Benny Goodman and Woody Herman; Bus Etri with Charlie Barnet's Orchestra; Bill De Arango for his recordings with Charlie Parker and Sarah Vaughan; Arv Garrison, Tony Rizzi, Gene Sargent for their work on the recording Five Guitars in Flight and Floyd Smith, Elmer Snowden, Bill Harris, Jimmy Gourley, Rene Thomas, Joe Puma, Al Harris and Harry Volpe; Howard Roberts, for his great Los Angeles studio work; Kenny Burrell, for his many solo albums; Chuck Wayne's guitar artistry with George Shearing; George Barnes, for his collaboration with Carl Kress and George Van Eps, master chord melody guitarist.

Other outstanding jazz guitarists are John Abercrombie, Lee Ritenour, Hy White, Earl Klugh, Jack Marshall, Dick McDonough, Larry Coryell, Hank Garland, Ralph Towner, Phil Upchurch, Jack Wilkins, Attila Zoller, Ed Bickert, Billy Bean, Luiz Bonfa, Baden Powell, Jerry Hahn, Mary Osborne, Al DiMeola, Joe Diorio and Ron Eschete.

APPENDIX

GUIDELINES FOR PLAYING AND LISTENING TO JAZZ GUITAR

Aural memory is the memory which enables us to hear music inwardly, replaying the sound sensations we have heard by prior listening experiences (vibrational frequencies of sound) called tone. Our musical personalities and taste are determined by what we have heard in performance and what our memory chooses to replay inwardly.

PERFORMANCE STANDARD

1) Craft

    A) Understanding the music

    B) Technique

    C) Well-developed ear

2) Awareness

3) Creativity

4) Spirit (emotional drive)

5) Desire to communicate

6) The audience's desire to understand

JAZZ (From folk music to art form)

The core of jazz is the improvised solo. Every jazz performance is focused on the improvisation.

BLUEPRINTS (The six blueprints most common in jazz)

1)	Blues	12-bar chord progression
2)	Standard	Broadway show tunes or pop song of the day
3)	Be-Bop	Standard tune progression re-used as a foundation for be-bop tune
4)	Free-Form	Tempo, harmonic rhythm, chord structure, sequence, mood, special scales
5)	Modal	Uncommon sequence of chords/simply structured chords
6)	Contemporary	Uncommon chord sequences, complex chord structures

ELEMENTS OF THE SOLO

Habits	Patterned disciplines
Clichés	Musical ideas that are an integral part of the player's style
Quotes	Melodic fragments for influential jazz players
Repairing errors	Slide from erroneous pitch to the note the player was hearing in his head
Originality	Spontaneous and material

STRUCTURES

The Tune (song)	Original composition/popular song
Melody	It talks to the listener
Rhythm	Structured rhythms/the beat
Harmony	Chord progressions/harmonic relationships
Song form	Verse, chorus - A B A, A A B A, A B C A
Tempo	Variations of speed/slow-medium-fast

THE LISTENER

Must be able to hear the improviser's spontaneous musical thoughts and get a feeling of transparent hearing and/or seeing the act of spontaneous creating.

LIST OF TABLES

TABLE I

Mechanics of Guitar Playing

TABLE II

Finger Board Chart

TABLE III

Musician's Symbol Diagram

TABLE IV

The Evolution Of Jazz Guitar

TABLE I
MECHANICS OF GUITAR PLAYING

Make sure that your instrument is in tune by tuning to a pitch pipe, piano or tuning trainer (electrical device now on the market).

Guitar Sounds   Compass Written

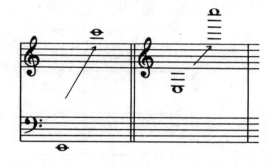

EXPLANATION OF SYMBOLS

a) Arabic numerals 1, 2, 3, and 4 refer to the fingers
   of the left hand.

b) The circle (o) indicates that the string is open.

c) Arabic numerals circled ③ indicate the
   string to be sounded.

d) This symbol ([ ) represents the barre,
   along with a left-hand fingering designation.

The BARRE (pronounced bar) is accomplished by pressing a finger across four or more strings.

e) The symbol "T" indicates the use of the thumb of
   the left hand to sound a note usually on the sixth string.

f) Defining a position of the left hand on the
   fingerboard is abbreviated to Pos, preceded by
   the number of the position in the form of a Roman numeral.

g) ⊓ = Down pick

    V = Up pick

TABLE II
FINGER BOARD CHART

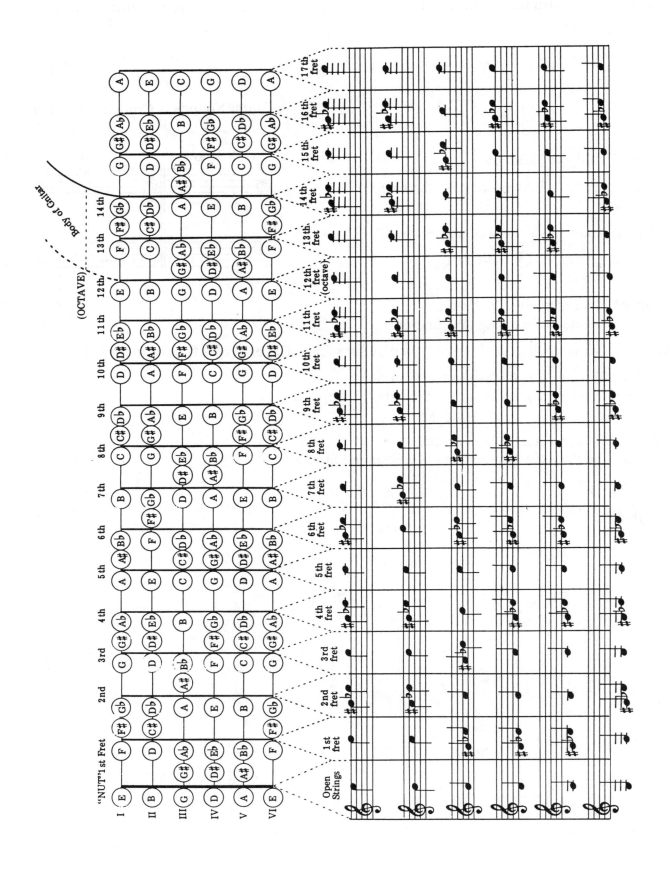

TABLE III
MUSICIAN'S SYMBOL DIAGRAM

The musician's script is his or her music sheet . . . It can range from a basic lead sheet with chord changes, to a full-blown score with every note appearing as it is played and dramatized. The following diagram shows you some of the symbols the musician works with.

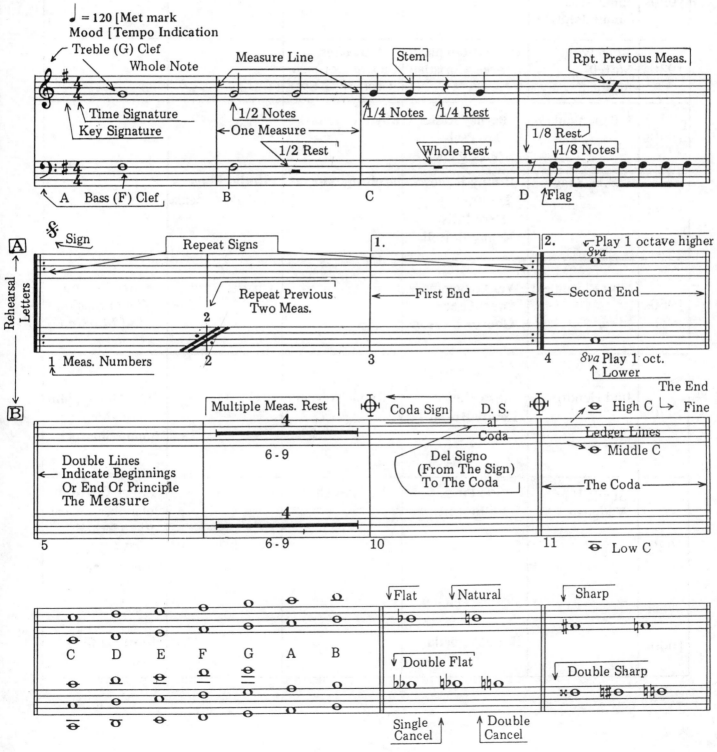

153

TABLE IV
THE EVOLUTION OF JAZZ GUITAR

	The Blues Tradition	Single-Note Horn Lines	Chordal Acoustic Sound	Influenced By Classical Music	Influenced By The Sound Of The Guitar In Rock And Pop Music
1920s	Leadbelly Blind Blake **Lonnie Johnson**		**Eddie Lang**		
1930s	Blind Willie McTell Big Bill Broonzy	**Django Reinhardt Charlie Christian**	**Carl Kress** Dick McDonough George Van Eps		
1940s	**T-Bone Walker**	**Barney Kessel** Les Paul George Barnes	**Rhythm Guitarists**		
1950s	B.B. King	**Jimmy Raney Tal Farlow** Herb Ellis Kenny Burrell	**Johnny Smith**	**Studio Players** Laurindo Almeida	
1960s	Mike Bloomfield	**Wes Montgomery** Grant Green **George Benson**		Charlie Byrd	Larry Coryell Gabor Szabo **Pat Martino**
1970s	Jimi Hendrix	**Jim Hall Lenny Breau**	Ralph Towner		**John McLaughlin** Al DiMeola Sonny Sharrock
1980s	Stevie Ray Vaughan	**Joe Pass** Ed Bickert	Earl Klugh		**Larry Carlton** John Abercrombie **Pat Metheny** Mike Stern Lee Ritenour
1990s		**Stanley Jordan**			**John Scofield** Bill Frisell

ABOUT THE RECORDING

In much the same way a painter uses different shading details to create atmosphere and drama, Jimmy has recorded each unique musical composition created for the guitar personality featured.

STAGE ONE: COMPOSING THE MUSIC

The *Complete Jazz Guitarist* recording was created in three stages: composing the music, sound design, and sound mixing. Stage one began with utilizing my Apophis Productions project studio. Using a Roland GR-1 guitar synthesizer and a Macintosh SE 30 computer, equipped with Finale 3.0 music software, I began to transcribe my improvised solos.

This music/publishing/transcribing/play back program, gave me complete control over every aspect of the music. I played around with each improvisation until it became a tune. Using Finales musical intelligence, I was able to hear, edit and print out each composition. All this recorded information was placed in a standard MIDI file for exporting to Opcode's 2.0 Vision sequencer.

TIP

To sum it up, it is best to play in your performance if you want it to sound realistic. A notation program is not designed to give you the energy level of a live sound.

STAGE TWO: SOUND DESIGN

Having finished sequencing each tune, I took my files to sound designer Marvin Sanders studio, located at the Bakery recording complex in Burbank, California. Each tune was scrutinized for its overall feel. As needed, we tweaked notes by modifying note velocities and durations. Once everything was together, we began to design a generic contemporary guitar sound.

Using a Roland Sound Canvas Mark II jazz guitar patch with a hard attack setting and blending it with a jazz guitar sound from a JU 880 wave form card, we created a composite sound for this project. However, one tune needed a distortion effect, so we picked the Boss SE 70 super effects processor for the job. After all this was accomplished, all the information was recorded on DAT.

TIP

Sounds that seem very good by themselves can take on a totally different personality when blended with other electronic sounds. It's important to keep an open ear, and listen very carefully to how sounds mix with each other as they are combined.

STAGE THREE: SOUND MIXING

Bakery staff engineer Michael James Greene and I have worked on a few projects together with great results. His process for mixing this music was first to preview the DAT information through the recording chain listening for any sonic problems. Michael then started to build our sound field by routing the dry signal into the recording console while contouring the sound with light equalization. As we were going through the process, the sounds were seasoned by reverberation and delays. While adjusting the balances, compression was added by using an insertion point in the recording chain. Then we adjusted the elements until the sounds were tasteful. This information was transferred to a Dawn Digital Work Station for assembly. Having finished this stage, a DAT master was made.

TIP

A good guitar sound requires a height, width, and depth in order to take on a living quality. Generally the longer the effect, like echo, delay and reverb, the farther back the sound goes. Height is controlled by the range of frequencies, from low to high and width by panning spread.

Even though you may have a strong background in the technical aspects of sound, you do not have to totally rely on them. I like to do things by instinct, if the music sounds right and feels right, it is right.

With a unique sound the jazz guitarist can sharply influence or totally change the listeners perception and experience.